ULTIMATE
BUYERS' GUIDE

Honda CBR900RR and CBR1000RR FireBlade

All models 1992 to 2008

Chris Horton

PMM Books

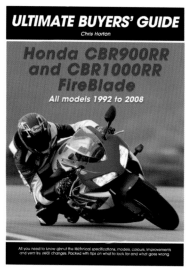

ULTIMATE BUYERS' GUIDE
Chris Horton

Honda CBR900RR
and CBR1000RR
FireBlade
All models 1992 to 2008

All you need to know about the technical specifications, models, colours, improvements and year by year changes. Packed with tips on what to look for and what goes wrong.

Copyright: Chris Horton, 2009

Photographs courtesy of Honda (UK) Ltd.; others by Peter Robain and the author
Edited by Peter Morgan
Design and layout by Sam Dorrington, SD Design

First published 2009

ISBN 978 0 954999 03 2

Published by PMM Books, an imprint of Peter Morgan Media Ltd.
PO Box 2561, Marlborough, Wiltshire, SN8 1YD, Great Britain.
Telephone: +44 1672 514038
E-mail: sales@pmmbooks.com
Website: www.pmmbooks.com

Printed in India by Replika Press Pvt. Ltd.

Contents

Honda CBR900RR and CBR1000RR FireBlade
All models 1992 to 2008

Welcome to the ever so slightly psychotic world of the Honda CBR900RR and CBR1000RR. Or the FireBlade as both machines are generically known – and almost obsessively loved – in many parts of the world.

Psychotic? You'd better believe it. Here's a so-called super-sports bike that weighs only about as much as three sacks of cement, packs a minimum of 124bhp (91kW), and in later versions as much as 180bhp (132kW), accelerates from standstill to 130mph (200kph) in around 10 seconds (with the front wheel in the air for most of that time, if you're brave and/or crazy enough), and will then rocket to around 170mph (275kph) or more.

Even with an 80kg (180lb) rider aboard you're talking about the same kind of power-to-weight ratio – if not quite the same aerodynamics, of course – as a modern Formula 1 car. It is *seriously* quick. No wonder that to date Honda has sold well over 32,000 FireBlades in the UK alone.

And then there's that name – FireBlade. Some say it's the result of a mistranslation from French to English for the Japanese word for lightning (which is actually either *denkou* or *raikou*), but it could hardly be more appropriate, immediately bringing to mind an image of some pyromaniac *samurai* swordsman. Perhaps not surprisingly in

the more politically correct United States (and certain other markets) it was originally badged simply CBR900RR. The subsequent larger-engined and more powerful models again (in the US, anyway) reflected merely the cylinder capacity rather than the bike's essential character: CBR918RR, CBR929RR, CBR954RR – and finally CBR1000RR.

But despite an emotive name it's a remarkably civilised machine, too. It's superbly built, and engineered to last. And it's comfortable enough to cover long distances at sensible and just about legal average speeds. Monumental fun, of course. And ultimately no more and no less psychotic than whoever happens to be twisting open the throttle at the time. You could even argue that with such huge reserves of power, grip and stopping ability it's actually one of the safest bikes on the road today. It's certainly one of the most evocative and inspiring.

Importantly, this book aims not to add to the burden of the would-be Blade buyer, but substantially to lighten it. We don't aim to theorise and pontificate about the bike's origins, or what might have been going through designer Tadao Baba's mind when he came up with the idea. (It's pretty obvious, really.) Within these pages, then, you'll find nothing but hard facts painstakingly gleaned from acknowledged FireBlade experts – and from

a number of long-standing and enthusiastic Blade owners, too. We've included a little history and background, certainly, but mainly just the kind of basic, no-nonsense information that as a would-be buyer you simply cannot afford to leave home without. There are production changes, colour schemes, and a very basic guide to chassis and engine serial numbers. And, of course, a comprehensive guide to the bike's few weaknesses (and its many strengths).

Please note, though, that of necessity we have based this book primarily around the UK-specification models. If you happen to be reading this in California or Queensland, then, and you a naturally wondering why the bikes that are on sale in your particular part of the world don't sound quite the same, year for year, as those that we have here in Britain, then I can only apologise. I'm confident that you'll still find the information extremely useful, though.

As for me, right now I'm off to buy a set of leathers and a new crash helmet, and then an early-model Blade of my very own. Just don't tell my wife or my mother, OK?

Chris Horton, Oxfordshire

HONDA CBR/FIREBLADE

Model	1992 (RR-N)	1993 (RR-P)	1994 (RR-R)	1995 (RR-S)	1996 (RR-T)	1997 (RR-V)
Bore/stroke (mm)	70.0 x 58.0	70.0 x 58.0	70.0 x 58.0	70.0 x 58.0	71.0 x 58.0	71.0 x 58.0
Capacity (cc)	893	893	893	893	918	918
Compression ratio	11.0:1	11.0:1	11.0:1	11.0:1	11.0:1	11.0:1
Maximum power (hp or kW/rpm)	124 (91)/10,500	124 (91)/10,500	124 (91)/10,500	124 (91)/10,500	128 (94)/10500	128 (94)/10500
Maximum torque (Nm or lbft/rpm)	88 (65)/8500	88 (65)/8500	88 (65)/8500	88 (65)/8500	91 (67)/8750	93 (69)/8500
Ignition system	Digital	Digital	Digital	Digital	Digital	Digital
Fuel/induction system	CV carburettors	CV carburettors	CV carburettors	CV carburettors	CV carburettors	CV carburettors
Gearbox	6-speed	6-speed	6-speed	6-speed	6-speed	6-speed
Front wheel	16-inch 6-spoke	16-inch 6-spoke	16-inch 6-spoke	16-inch 6-spoke	16-inch 6-spoke	16-inch 6-spoke
Front tyre size	130/70ZR16	130/70ZR16	130/70ZR16	130/70ZR16	130/70ZR16	130/70ZR16
Front disc (rotor) diameter (mm/ins)	296/11.7	296/11.7	296/11.7	296/11.7	296/11.7	296/11.7
Rear wheel	17-inch 6-spoke	17-inch 6-spoke	17-inch 6-spoke	17-inch 6-spoke	17-inch 6-spoke	17-inch 6-spoke
Rear tyre size	180/55ZR17	180/55ZR17	180/55ZR17	180/55ZR17	180/55ZR17	180/55ZR17
Rear disc (rotor) diameter (mm/ins)	220/8.7	220/8.7	220/8.7	220/8.7	220/8.7	220/8.7
Dimensions L x W x H (mm)	2135/685/1115	2135/685/1115	2135/685/1130	2135/685/1130	2135/675/1130	2135/675/1130
Dimensions L x W x H (ins)	84.0/27.0/43.9	84.0/27.0/43.9	84.0/27.0/43.9	84.0/27.0/43.9	84.0/26.6/43.0	84.0/27.0/43.9
Wheelbase (mm/ins)	1405/55.3	1405/55.3	1405/55.3	1405/55.3	1405/55.3	1405/55.3
Seat height (mm/ins)	770/30.3	770/30.3	770/30.3	800/31.5	810/31.9	810/31.9
Ground clearance (mm/ins)	130/5.1	130/5.1	130/5.1	130/5.1	140/5.5	140/5.5
Fuel capacity (litres/US gallons)	18/4.77	18/4.77	18/4.77	18/4.77	18/4.77	18/4.77
Dry weight (kg/lb)	185/408	185/408	185/408	185/408	183/404	183/404
Power/weight (hp/kW per tonne)	670/492	670/492	670/492	670/492	700/514	700/514
Maximum speed (mph/kph)	149/239	160/257	155/249	161/258	163/261	163/261
Notes	Engine layout: water-cooled, double-overhead-camshaft, tranversely mounted four cylinder (all models) Transmission: wet-type multi-plate clutch with coil springs; chain drive to rear wheel					

1998 (RR-W)	1999 (RR-X)	2000 (RR-Y)	2001 (RR-1)	2002 (RR-2)	2003 (RR-3)
71.0 x 58.0	71.0 x 58.0	74.0 x 54.0	74.0 x 54.0	75.0 x 54.0	75.0 x 54.0
918	918	929	929	954	954
11.1:1	11.1:1	11.3:1	11.3:1	11.5:1	11.5:1
128 (94)/10,500	130 (95)/10,500	152 (111)/11,000	152 (111)/11,000	152 (111)/11,250	152 (111)/11,250
91 (69)/8500	92 (68)/8500	103 (76)/9000	101 (xxx)/9000	104 (77)/9500	105(78)/9500
Digital	Computerised	Computerised	Computerised	Computerised	Computerised
CV carburettors	CV carburettors	PGM-FI	PGM-FI	PGM-FI	PGM-FI
6-speed	6-speed	6-speed	6-speed	6-speed	6-speed
16-inch 6-spoke	16-inch 6-spoke	17-inch 3-spoke	17-inch 3-spoke	17-inch 3-spoke	17-inch 3-spoke
130/70ZR16	130/70ZR16	120/70ZR17	120/70ZR17	120/70ZR17	120/70ZR17
310/12.2	310/12.2	310/12.2	310/12.2	310/12.2	310/12.2
17-inch 6-spoke	17-inch 6-spoke	17-inch 3-spoke	17-inch 3-spoke	17-inch 3-spoke	17-inch 3-spoke
180/55ZR17	180/55ZR17	190/50ZR17	190/50ZR17	190/50ZR17	190/50ZR17
220/8.7	220/8.7	220/8.7	220/8.7	220/8.7	220/8.7
2135/685/1135	2040/685/1135	2065/680/1125	2065/680/1125	2025/680/1135	2025/680/1135
84.0/27.0/43.9	84.0/27.0/43.9	84.0/27.0/43.9	84.0/26.6/43.0	79.7/26.8/44.7	79.7/26.8/44.7
1405/55.3	1405/55.3	1400/55.1	1400/55.1	1400/55.1	1400/55.1
810/31.9	810/31.9	815/32.1	815/32.1	815/32.1	820/32.3
140/5.5	140/5.5	140/5.5	130/5.1	130/5.1	130/5.1
18/4.77	18/4.77	18/4.77	18/4.77	18/4.77	18/4.77
180/397	180/397	170/375	170/375	168/370	168/370
711/522	722/528	894/653	894/653	905/661	905/661
166/266	171/274	175/280	175/280	n/a	n/a

Carburation types: CV = constant vacuum (carburettor); PGM-FI = fuel injection; PGM-DSFI = dual sequential fuel injection

Model	2004 (RR-4)	2005 (RR-5)	2006 (RR-6)	2007 (RR-7)	2008 (RR-8)
Bore/stroke (mm)	75.0/56.5	75.0/56.5	75.0/56.5	75.0/56.5	76.0/55.1
Capacity (cc)	998	998	998	998	1000
Compression ratio	11.9:1	11.9:1	11.9:1	12.2:1	12.3:1
Maximum power (hp or kW/rpm)	172 (126)/11,250	172 (126)/11,250	170 (124)/11,250	173 (126)/12,500	175 (130)/12,000
Maximum torque (Nm or lbft/rpm)	115 (78)/8500	115 (78)/8500	115 (78)/8500	115 (85)/10000rpm	112 (83)/8500rpm
Ignition system	Computerised	Computerised	Computerised	Computerised	Computerised
Fuel/induction system	PGM-DSFI	PGM-DSFI	PGM-DSFI	PGM-DSFI	PGM-DSFI
Gearbox	6-speed	6-speed	6-speed	Six-speed	6-speed
Front wheel	17-inch 3-spoke	17-inch 3-spoke	17-inch 3-spoke	17-inch 3-spoke	17-inch 3-spoke
Front tyre size	120/70ZR17	120/70ZR17	120/70ZR17	120/70ZR17	120/70ZR17
Front disc (rotor) diameter (mm/ins)	310/12.2	310/12.2	320/12.6	320/12.6	320/12.6
Rear wheel	17-inch 3-spoke	17-inch 3-spoke	17-inch 3-spoke	17-inch 3-spoke	17-inch 3-spoke
Rear tyre size	190/50ZR17	190/50ZR17	190/50ZR17	190/50ZR17	190/50ZR17
Rear disc (rotor) diameter (mm/ins)	220/8.7	220/8.7	220/8.7	220/8.7	220/8.7
Dimensions L x W x H (mm)	2025/720/1120	2025/720/1120	2025/720/1120	2030/720/1118	2080/685/1130
Dimensions L x W x H (ins)	79.7/28.4/44.1	79.7/28.4/44.1	79.7/28.4/44.1	79.9/28.4/44.0	81.9/27.0/44.5
Wheelbase (mm/ins)	1410/55.5	1410/55.5	1410/55.5	1410/55.5	1410/55.5
Seat height (mm/ins)	820/32.3	820/32.3	820/32.3	831/32.7	820/32.3
Ground clearance (mm/ins)	130/5.1	130/5.1	130/5.1	130/5.1	130/5.1
Fuel capacity (litres/US gallons)	18/4.77	18/4.77	18/4.77	18/4.77	17.7/4.7
Dry weight (kg/lbs)	179/395	179/395	179/395	176/388	172/379
Power/weight (hp or kW/tonne)	961/704	961/704	949/693	983/716	1035/762
Maximum speed (mph/kph)	n/a	n/a	n/a	n/a	n/a
Notes	*Engine layout:* water-cooled, double-overhead-camshaft, tranversely mounted four cylinder (all models) *Transmission:* wet-type multi-plate clutch with coil springs, chain drive to rear wheel *Carburation types:* CV = constant vacuum (carburettor); PGM-FI = fuel injection; PGM-DSFI = dual sequential fuel injection				

Given the benefit of 20/20 hindsight, even the very first Honda CBR900RR FireBlade today seems an obvious modern classic. How – with the muscular grunt of a 1.0-litre sports bike in a chassis no bigger or heavier than that of a typical 600cc machine – could it possibly fail to be?

Compact, light, and breathtakingly agile, it offered – as even the earliest models still do today – immense straight-line performance, razor-sharp handling, race-grade braking, Honda's legendary build-quality and reliability, and perhaps most significantly looked for all the world as if it had just taken the chequered flag at Daytona or Jarama. A competition bike with lights and a licence plate is how many described it, and they weren't too far from the truth.

But this was in early 1992. The world was in the iron grip of an economic recession. The stock market was falling like a stone. Interest rates were off the scale. Prestige-car and motorcycle dealerships, which a few years earlier had been selling their wares by the truckload, were running out of space to store cancelled orders. Everywhere you looked, homeowners were struggling to keep massive mortgages afloat against a rising tide of lay-offs, negative equity and foreclosures. The last thing we all needed, you might have concluded, was a 124bhp (91kW) superbike, with a rear tyre broader than the average car's, and capable of more than double the highway speed limit. The popular press had a field day.

Yet somehow the FireBlade caught the mood of the moment. After all, aspirations don't disappear just because you can't immediately fulfill them – and man has long had a seemingly insatiable need for speed. And speed was just one of many things the Blade could always deliver in glorious abundance.

OK, so you could buy a nice, sensible family car for not much more, and whichever way you looked at it, this bike was really just an indulgence. But what the heck? You had a bit of cash put aside, you could work some overtime, and just about afford to put the rest on finance. And you only live once, anyway. (Which, sadly, for many over-confident Blade owners wasn't for long. Not for nothing did the early models – not entirely justifiably – become known as the Widowmaker.) Whatever the reason, whatever

All Blades are light, agile, and breathtakingly quick; not for the faint-hearted

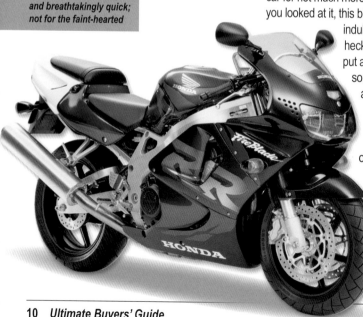

CERTAINTY

Will you be able to insure it? Check before you buy, not after...

its qualities, the FireBlade almost immediately became *the* really quick sports machine to have. For those who knew their high-performance bikes – and for many others who simply wanted to don brightly coloured leathers and look the part – the CBR900RR-N, as it was way back then, was a must-have fashion accessory.

'It seemed like there were hundreds of them on the Isle of Man in '92 and '93,' recalled one independent dealer to the author not so long ago. 'And one in every hedge, where some over-ambitious soul had gone off. It wasn't until about 1998 that bikes like the [Yamaha] R1 really started to outnumber it.'

The CBR900 sold better than its creators could have dreamed, and evolved into a whole hierarchy; a sort of two-wheeled Porsche 911. Then and now the Blade family are still best-sellers across the planet. It's not bad at all for a bike that first started to take shape the best part of two decades ago.

Having reinvented the wheel, as it were – and certainly having offered the first of a whole new generation of super-sports bikes – Honda had plainly taken its rivals completely by surprise. The FireBlade's first serious threat in terms of engine power was the Suzuki GSXR750, launched fully four years later, in 1996, and Yamaha's challenger, the previously mentioned 998cc R1, appeared only as recently as 1998. Kawasaki's first real contender was the 899cc ZX9, but that was widely considered to be more large sports tourer than genuine superbike, and the cognoscenti voted with their chequebooks – even if the Honda, to those enthusiasts' equally obvious disdain, was itself becoming a little less extreme during this period.

And all this was in spite of a surprisingly slow evolutionary process for the FireBlade. Between the 1992-season RR-N models and the 1995 RR-S (we'll explain these seemingly mysterious but actually quite logical designations later)

the high-profile Honda's only significant update was the introduction of so-called fox-eye headlamps and some rather wild new colour schemes, the latter known as the Urban Tiger range, for 1994. Indeed, it was only for the 1996 model year's RR-T bikes that engine capacity and power saw their first boost – to 918cc and 128bhp (94kW), respectively.

The next major change came in 1997, when the RR-W models gained restyled body panels and a digital engine-temperature gauge – but no more power. That same period saw the Yamaha R1 well and truly steal the Blade's thunder, too, with its fulsome 998cc and 150bhp (110kW), and rather surprisingly it took Honda until the 2000 season to fight back with a major facelift. But this saw the Blade's engine pushed up to 929cc (with a bigger bore and stroke) and no less than 152bhp (111kW). These RR-Y models also benefited from a 17-inch front wheel instead of the previous 16-inch rim (which, although it had contributed in no small measure to the Blade's extraordinary agility, also made it rather twitchy), and so-called upside-down front forks. (More on these later.)

Since then a more or less biennial update programme has seen the FireBlade maintain and even extend its competitive edge, once again becoming the super-sports bike by which all others are judged – and without doubt remaining both a technological *tour de force* and a modern classic. The 2001 RR-1, for instance, offered only detail improvements, but then in 2002 the RR-2 models brought not only another useful rise in engine size and power (954cc, 147bhp/108kW) but also a visual facelift.

For 2003 the RR-3 again received little more than new colours, but then in 2004 the RR-4's engine was pushed right up to 998cc, in an obvious head-to-head clash with both Ducati and Yamaha. No less important, the Honda, by now known technically (but not nearly as entertainingly) as the CBR1000RR, gained a race-style, under-seat exhaust system. Whatever the now familiar name on the side of the fairing might have suggested, it was effectively a brand-new bike from the wheels up.

In 2005 came the RR-5 models, and then for 2006 – surprise, surprise – the RR-6, with what amounted to another new engine offering a claimed 170bhp (125kW) at the crankshaft. This was sufficient to propel a modern CBR at up to 177mph (283kph), and decisively returned it to its (many say rightful) place as the hooligan's bike *par excellence*.

The 2007 season brought with it only a number of relatively modest improvements – among them a new paint job and minor tweaks underneath, including two fuel injectors per cylinder for a smoother throttle response, a competition-style cassette-type gearset, and not least a catalytic converter to keep the environmentalists just a little happier.

The 2008-season CBR1000RR models brought with them yet another major redesign, and yet another new beginning in the seemingly unstoppable CBR story. There was a new and externally more compact engine, with capacity squeezed out to 999.8cc, an easier-to-use clutch, the next generation of Honda's Electronic Steering Damper (HESD), and a shorter wheelbase – all clothed in lower drag, slimmer bodywork. It has been a genuinely relentless development story.

The Blade has become ever more affordable, too. Here in Britain back in 1992 the RR-N models started at a sizeable £7125, while in the USA owners benefited more from almost 'dollars for pounds' pricing that kept the CBR1000 well under ten grand. Inevitably the price rose steadily through the rest of the 1990s, but it's a fact that today (mid-2008), a CBR1000RR would still cost you only £9300 in the UK, and an even more impressive $11,599 in the USA.

In car terms you would need to spend roughly ten times that amount on, say, a Porsche 911 GT3 to obtain similar performance. And even that four-wheeled automotive icon is by no means immune to the effects of depreciation, which – perhaps unsurprisingly – seems to affect the Honda rather less than most of its kind.

Race-honed chassis makes the FireBlade an ideal trackday bike

FireBlade: the affordable classic

There have been used FireBlades on the market for very nearly as long as brand-new ones. The irony within that situation, of course, is that having become acknowledged modern classics, the good ones, and particularly the good early ones, are always in frustratingly short supply – with an obvious effect on prices relative to what might be termed their real value. Finding a good early model with a sensible distance reading can be quite hard work, in other words, and the prices generally being asked reflect both the limited supply and the high demand. If you find a good one, then, don't let it slip through your fingers!

What it really means, not least because brand-new bikes are (relatively!) inexpensive, is that you'll be able to afford a much more recent machine than you might have expected. Indeed, we would go as far as to suggest that beyond their certain curiosity value (and an undeniable kudos on the street) there's actually very little technical merit in going for a particularly early bike – a pre-1994 machine, in other words.

The later ones are not only likely to have fewer miles on the clock, but should also exhibit fewer of the not exactly numerous problems known to afflict the FireBlade. And if nothing else they will come with quite a lot more in the way of features and equipment.

It's your call, and you may actively want an early bike, of course, but you certainly shouldn't ignore the later ones.

The next big surprise is that the FireBlade doesn't require constant and highly specialised maintenance. Its engine may by supercar standards be a tiny, highly stressed unit (current models will rev to 12,000rpm or more), but it was built to take the punishment

Honda knew that its likely buyers would routinely dish out. Most experts agree that a service every year or 4000 miles (6500km) is about right (superbikes, used essentially as elaborate playthings, tend to cover rather lower annual mileages than cars). The engine's valve clearances need to be checked and if necessary manually adjusted every 16,000 miles (25,000km), and the brake pads and discs checked and replaced as necessary. It's predictably easy to see – and feel – when that might be.

One of the bigger running costs once you've bought your bike is going to be tyres. A decent rear cover should – we repeat: should – last for about 3000 miles, but obviously rather less than that if you habitually use the blistering acceleration to the full (which will have a similar effect on the chain and sprockets, too), or if you choose a particularly grippy make. Bridgestone, Pirelli, Michelin and Dunlop are all highly regarded, widely available, either online or from specialist fitters, and often for much less than the manufacturers' retail figures. Shop around. But don't skimp on this or any other safety-related area. Your life depends on it.

This leads us rather neatly to what is probably the most obvious, but at the same time useful, piece of general advice for any would-be FireBlade owner.

The FireBlade really is one seriously rapid piece of kit. Even the earliest models are capable of well over double most countries' open highway speed limits (on a private circuit, of course…), and the later ones run intoxicatingly close to 200mph (320kph). Performance of that calibre is most definitely not for the faint-hearted or the inexperienced. You have been warned!

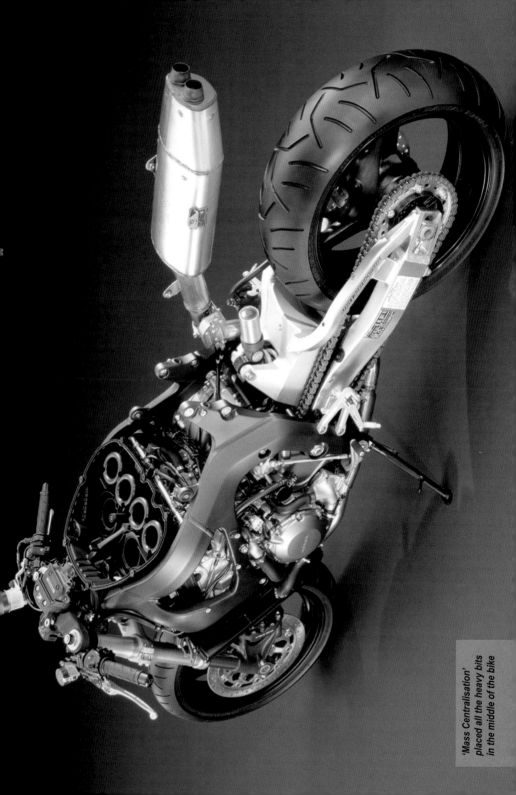

'Mass Centralisation' placed all the heavy bits in the middle of the bike

Choosing and owning a FireBlade

Very high performance places an enormous load on just about every part of the machine, and particularly on the tyres, the brakes and the final drive (the chain and the two sprockets, in other words). That in itself isn't a major problem – they can all be renewed relatively simply and cheaply, especially if you're used to the complexities of high-performance cars – but the plain truth is that many of the older bikes you see for sale today could well have led very hard lives, indeed, and as they've fallen into the hands of perhaps less caring and less affluent owners may well have been both neglected and even willfully abused. And while some 'abuse' is both obvious and to an extent forgivable – who could buy a FireBlade and then not want to find out how quick it is? – the problem is

that you have no effective way of telling if the engine has been routinely red-lined, maybe even from stone-cold. It really is a case of buyer beware, and/or being extremely choosy about who you buy from.

Crash damage is a big issue, too. We'll cover the specifics you need to look for a little later, but it's enough to say here that with a front wheel all too ready to head skyward, and with rather too many riders insufficiently talented to cope with the phenomenon, a great many FireBlades have suffered some sort of coming-together with the ground. Or maybe something even less forgiving.

The good news, if such it can be called, is that many a scrape is just that: an irritating cosmetic issue rather than a catastrophe. Misaligned or bent forks, distorted frames,

Latest bike looks radically different – but still every inch a modern classic

and even elliptical or cracked wheels are by no means uncommon, but can often be difficult to spot. For that reason alone you must be prepared either to pay your money and take your chance (which is fair enough if you're buying from a reputable source, such as an official Honda dealer or a recognised independent), or else to seek out the advice of an acknowledged expert.

No less unsurprisingly the FireBlade has always been vulnerable to theft. To be fair, Honda has always equipped it with reasonable-quality locks, and from the 1998 model year an electronic immobiliser. Even so, a bike this valuable, this popular, this saleable – and this light – will always be an easy target for the determined felon.

As an owner you'll have to devise your own additional security measures, but as a potential buyer you have to be absolutely certain that whoever is selling your chosen bike really does have the legal title to do so. Here in the UK there are some fairly well-known steps that you can take to safeguard yourself (not least an HPI or DVLA check; see the Contacts section at the end of the

It's not just from a distance that the FireBlade looks superb; detail fit and finish are excellent

book for details). Once again the most obvious advice has to be that you buy only from a recognised and reputable source such as a dealer with proper premises – and not some nameless individual you met in some equally nameless bar or gas station.

Colours best described as 'bright'; it's all part of the image, though!

And do remember that a machine of this kind runs on rather more than fresh air. In high-performance-car terms it's an absolute bargain, both to buy and then to maintain. But the fact is that if you use your FireBlade as enthusiastically as its wonderful engine and chassis will encourage you to, then it does have a bit of a thirst. Expect to see as little as 20 miles to the Imperial gallon (17 miles/US gallon, 14.1l/100km) from the typically 18-litre/4.8 US gallon tank if you ride it hard.

Don't forget to budget for insurance. Have the right kind of driving record and it can be almost absurdly inexpensive for the level of performance the FireBlade offers. If you have the wrong kind of record, however, you might not be able to buy cover at any price. It's certainly worth

Special editions like this rare Repsol replica are naturally sought-after

obtaining some typical quotes before you buy your bike rather than afterwards.

Bear in mind, too, that the FireBlade is by its nature one of those bikes that people love to modify (and the fact that it's so eminently tunable is one of its many attractions, in any case). For the purposes of this book, though, we have to assume that you are inspecting more-or-less standard machines – or, if not, that you know exactly what you're doing, in which case you obviously won't need us to tell you. It's impossible for us to guess how owners might have mixed and matched bits and pieces, and all we can suggest is once again that you consult an expert. Most Honda bike dealerships seem to have at least one Blade addict on the premises, whether in the sales department or toiling away in the workshop, and such is the nature of the beast – the bike, that is – that they will more often than not be delighted to share their knowledge.

Is it for you?

ast but not least, we have to question – or prompt you to ask yourself, anyway – whether this really is the bike for you. That might sound a strange idea to suggest in a book of this nature, but the FireBlade – and lots of other machines like it – is always going to be something of an acquired taste.

The riding position is fairly uncompromising, for a start, and while that may not be a big issue if you're using your Blade simply for short joyrides, an aching neck, shoulders and back will soon let you know when you've exceeded your own design limits. Even those who love their Blades with a passion beyond reason concede that you need to be doing at least 80mph (130kph) for the oncoming air to take at least some of the strain off your upper

body, and in many parts of the world that's just not going to happen very often – if at all if you value your driver's licence.

We also have to assume that you have at least some knowledge of buying high-performance motor vehicles in general; or else that you will, as we suggested a moment ago, be seeking independent (but above all genuinely knowledgeable) expert advice.

A bike – even one as fast and as complex as this – is a remarkably straightforward device compared to a typical modern sports car, and we're happy that in this buyers' guide we have covered just about every necessary area. As ever, though, there can be no substitute for genuine, hands-on experience – either your own, or that of someone you know you can trust.

For Honda, like most of the major vehicle manufacturers, there is a small but important difference between calendar years and model years. The model year usually – but not invariably – starts in November or December of the previous calendar year, but can begin as early as September. This explains why what is known officially as, say, a 1998-model bike could have been sold and registered during the latter part of 1997. It will also be apparent from what follows that, whether initially by accident or by design, the CBR has in practice undergone a programme of basically two-yearly upgrades and improvements since its launch back in 1992.

SPRING 1989

Disillusioned by the then current crop of sports bikes, veteran Honda designer Tadao Baba (below) sets out to come up with a completely new kind of machine: light and powerful and thus exciting, but at the same time as agile and as easy to ride as possible. It must also put into practice his strongly held views on what comes to be known throughout the CBR world as Mass Centralisation, whereby the heaviest parts of the machine are positioned as close as practicable to its central point.

1992 MODEL YEAR

The first CBR – the 893cc, 124bhp (91kW) CBR900RR-N – is unveiled. Features include aggressive super-sports bodywork highlighted by a distinctive tiger-stripe colour scheme (in either Black or Ross White), a light and rigid twin-spar aluminium frame, cartridge-type front forks with lightweight lower sections, a so-called Yagura-style swinging arm with a remote hydraulic-damper reservoir, and powerful four-piston front brake calipers with 296mm (11.65in) 'floating' discs (rotors).

The engine – an entirely new in-line four – has a two-piece, horizontally split crankcase and new slipper-style pistons, and new 38mm (1.5in) slant-type constant-vacuum carburettors. Demand soon outstrips supply – despite a deep worldwide economic recession.

1993 MODEL YEAR

The CBR900RR-P models, also 893cc and 124bhp (91kW), are unveiled, with colour schemes essentially as per the previous year's bikes.

1994 MODEL YEAR

The FireBlade's first major revision gives it restyled front bodywork for the 1994-season CB900RR-R models – the so-called and now familiar 'fox-eye' headlamps, behind a one-piece, flush-fitting lens – and a new range of bold Urban Tiger colour schemes, as they're known. (Technically, it's Sandy Beige Metallic. You could also have Ross White or Sparkler Black Pearl.) There is also a new and lighter magnesium cylinder-head cover, new fully adjustable front forks, and not least a new aluminium-finish exhaust silencer. But capacity and power output remain as before, at 893cc and 124bhp (91kW), respectively.

1995 MODEL YEAR

The RR-S models are announced, still with 893cc and 124bhp (91kW), and still with essentially the same colour schemes as the previous year. But there's a slight adjustment to the riding position – the seat height is now 800mm (31.5in) rather than the previous 770mm (30.3in), for instance.

1996 MODEL YEAR

The 1996-season RR-T models (known as the CBR918RR in the US) gain an all-new 918cc, 128bhp (94kW) engine with a computerised, map-type ignition system and a new stainless-steel exhaust with a canister-style aluminium silencer. The frame is a new twin-spar, triple-box-section item in aluminium, with thinner walls than before, and the swinging arm is a redesigned and more robust Yagura unit. The redesigned main fairing and front mudguard are thinner and lighter, too.

Suspension upgrades and further adjustments to the riding position (the seat height is now 810mm, 31.9in) make the bike rather less racer-like, and a little more civilised (to the obvious disgust of hard-core CBR fans). Colour schemes are Black, Blitz Grey Metallic, and Sparkling Red.

1997 MODEL YEAR

The 1997-model RR-V is remarkably (some would say disappointingly) little changed compared to the previous model, but thanks to an aluminium exhaust silencer is slightly lighter than the previous year's models. The only other news is a range of updated colour schemes: Black, Pearl Citron Yellow, and the old favourite, Ross White.

1998 MODEL YEAR

In response to Yamaha's then-new R1 the 1998-model RR-W gains a redesigned fairing and headlamp, claimed to have a lower drag coefficient than before, and a broader combined seat/tail-light unit. The engine is still 918cc, and despite a number of detail improvements still offers 128bhp (94kW), but the figures suggest marginally less torque than the previous year – 91Nm (67lbft) rather than 93Nm (69lbft). Other changes include a new fully electronic instrument panel, an anti-theft immobiliser (Honda Ignition Security System, or HISS), new front brake calipers and larger-diameter (310mm, 12.2in) floating front brake rotors, and a redesigned, tapered box-section swinging arm that's claimed to be more rigid than previously. Even so, the motorcycle press rather harshly labels the new bike a sports tourer. Colour schemes are Black, Candy Blaze Orange, and Sparkling Red.

1999 MODEL YEAR

The RR-X models are announced for the 1999 model year. There are no significant changes, although the 918cc engine now offers marginally more power and torque. Colours are Jerez Blue Metallic, Lapis Blue Metallic, and once again Sparkling Red.

2000 MODEL YEAR

The world may have been scaring itself witless about the millennium bug, but for the 2000 season Honda comes up with the significantly revised RR-Y models (CBR929RR in the US). There's an all-new PGM-FI fuel-injected 929cc engine with a so-called bypass starter for quicker and easier starting, at 170kg (375lb) they're 10kg (22lb) lighter than the previous season's bikes, and come with no less than 152bhp (111kW) and 103Nm (76lbft). German-market models get a new HECS3 low-emissions system. There's also a new exhaust with H-TEV (Honda Titanium Exhaust Valve) for improved high-speed performance. The frame is a redesigned twin-spar aluminium unit that's said to be both lighter and stiffer than before, and the fairing is a distinctive new unit with sharper and more compact styling; the headlight is a new three-bulb system. The RR-Y also gains upside-down 43mm (1.7in) front forks, a 17-inch triple-spoke front wheel (and wider tyre) in place of the previous 16-inch item (the rear wheel is a three-spoke item, too), and not least an unmistakably squarer appearance. The seat height rises to 815mm (32in). The HISS security system is improved, too. Colours are Black, Sunrise Yellow, and Winning Red.

2001 MODEL YEAR

There are no big changes for the 2001 season – not surprising, really, after the major modifications of a year earlier – other than a new model-designation system. Under this the current bike is now known technically as the CBR900RR-1 (although it's still the CBR929RR in the US). Colours are Italian Red, Lapis Blue Metallic, and Pearl Flash Yellow, together with a special edition that rejoices in the name of Accurate Silver Metallic.

2002 MODEL YEAR

The 2002-model RR-2 gains not only an all-new, fuel-injected 954cc engine (for which reason the bike is known as the CBR954RR in the US), but also a much sleeker, tougher stance thanks to changes to every body panel. Bigger fuel injectors and greater processing capacity from the engine management system boost power and torque to 149bhp (109kW) and 104Nm (77lbft), respectively. A stronger frame and headstock, together with a more rigid aluminium swinging arm, gives improved handling, and at a new low weight of 168kg (370lb) the bike isn't just lighter than the competition, but even weighs less than Honda's own CBR600. Available in Pearl Flash Yellow, Ross White or Winning Red, it's reckoned by many enthusiasts to be the best-looking CBR since the 1994 'fox-eye' Urban Tiger model.

2003 MODEL YEAR

Mechanically and structurally the 2003 RR-3 models are much as the 2002 bikes, but the colour schemes get a modest makeover: Black is joined by Black and Yellow, and also Candy Tahitian Blue. CBR enthusiasts around the world mourn the retirement of designer Tadao Baba, no doubt wondering what effect this might have on future models.

2004 MODEL YEAR

Notwithstanding Tadao Baba's retirement the previous season, the biggest programme of upgrades and improvements in 13 years gives the 2004-model RR-4 FireBlade (CBR1000RR in both the European and US markets) a new 998cc, 178bhp (130kW) engine with two-stage Dual Sequential Fuel Injection (PGM-DSFI) and a ram-air induction system. The frame is a new die-cast aluminium item based on Honda's RC211V Moto GP-winning bike, with a new Unit Pro-Link swinging arm, upside-down 43mm (1.7in) HMAS cartridge-type front forks, and new radially mounted front brake calipers. The clutch is now hydraulically actuated rather than by the previous cable. There's also a race-style, under-seat exhaust system, a slightly longer

wheelbase – 1410mm (55.5in) instead of 1400 (55.1in) – and Honda's self-adjusting electronic steering damper (HESD). This last feature is a first for a road bike. Visually the RR-4 – badged, logically enough, as the CBR1000RR – resembles Honda's RC211 V5 racer, and although at 179kg (395lb) it's 11kg (24lb) heavier than the previous year's model is said still to embody to the full Honda's famous philosophy of Mass Centralisation. Colours are Black and Winning Red, and there's also another brand-new scheme in the form of Pearl Fadeless White.

2005 MODEL YEAR

The 2005-model RR-5 is much as the previous year's RR-4, with 998cc and 178bhp (130kW). The strictly limited-edition Repsol replica, painted in what's known rather poetically as Pearl Siren Blue-A, is highly sought after by enthusiasts today.

Other colours are Black, Candy Tahitian Blue, and not least Winning Red.

2006 MODEL YEAR

The 2006-model RR-6 benefits from yet another ambitious programme of upgrades, resulting in lower weight, more power and better handling, according to Honda. The engine remains at 998cc and 178bhp (130kW), but there are many detail changes, including new cylinder-head ports and combustion chambers, new inlet camshaft and valves, and a higher rev limit. A new clutch, bearings and gears between them improve the transmission. The chassis geometry is modified (with revised settings for the front suspension), and larger (320mm, 12.6in) front rotors with four-piston calipers improve the stopping power. Cosmetically the bike gains all-new bodywork for an aggressive, race-ready look, and better seat foam for improved long-distance comfort. Colour schemes are Graphite Black, Winning Red, and the intriguingly titled Iron Nail Silver Metallic-U.

2007 MODEL YEAR

The 2007 season brings with it a programme of modest but none the less effective improvements rather than large-scale changes. The engine, still at 998cc and 178bhp (130kW), retains its PGM-DSFI Dual Sequential Fuel Injection system, but now has two injectors per cylinder for a smoother throttle response, and the under-seat exhaust is not only slightly lighter than previously but also gains for the first time a catalytic converter (and thus requiring the use of unleaded fuel). The radiator, too, is narrower than before, and thus lighter. The transmission has a race-style cassette-type gearset, and the previously 40-tooth primary drive sprocket gains an additional two teeth for improved acceleration. Chassis-wise, the steering head's caster angle and trail are reduced in order to reduce slightly the effort required for steering. Colour schemes are Graphite Black, Pearl Fadeless White (in tricolour form with Pearl Siren Blue and Winning Red highlights), and Winning Red.

2008 MODEL YEAR

Yet another stunning redesign in the continuing and seemingly unstoppable evolution of the CBR. A brand-new engine design sees capacity edged up to fully 1000cc (actually, it's 999.8cc, but what's 0.2cc between friends?), with maximum power now a muscular 180bhp (132kW). There's a new, lighter-action slipper clutch, and a revised HESD steering damper. There's also all-new and slimmer bodywork with an underslung and very stylish exhaust, but the already excellent suspension is carried over. Losing 6kg (13lb) to an overall 199kg (439lb), this CBR – still known technically as the CBR10000RR – claims to have the best power-to-weight ratio in the superbike class.

Frame and engine numbers

t was originally planned to include in this Ultimate Buyers' Guide a complete worldwide VIN (Vehicle Identification Number) decoder for all CBR/FireBlade models to date, but it soon became obvious that this would be far too complex and unwieldy for a book of this scope. That said, even the most cursory glance at the industry-standard sequence of letters and digits stamped directly into the frame on either the left or later the right side of the steering head, and on earlier bikes repeated on a riveted-on plate nearby, will tell

you quite a lot about the machine in question. Or it certainly should, anyway.

From the 1992 RR-N models, for instance, up to and including the 1995-season RR-S machines, the VIN is prefixed SC28. The engine number, stamped on the top right-hand side of the crankcase, just inboard of the clutch housing (and assuming that it's still the original power unit, of course) should be prefixed SC28E.

For the 1996 through 1999 model years inclusive these prefixes became SC33A for the frame, and SC33E for the engine. For the 2000

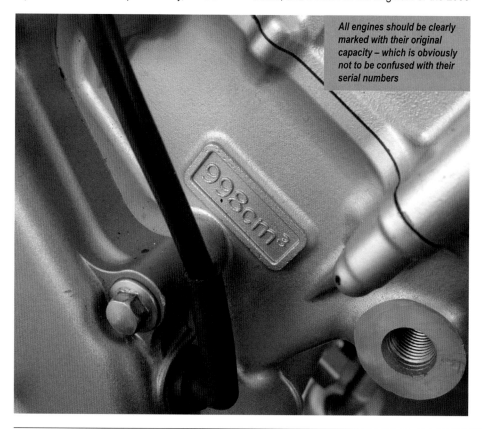

All engines should be clearly marked with their original capacity – which is obviously not to be confused with their serial numbers

SC28-2351209

Frame number is on either the left or later the right side of the steering head, and also a riveted-on plate

E 13

10 01652
78 01658

HONDA MOTOR CO., LTD. TOKYO JAPAN
TYP
TYPE   SC28
GENRE   NO.
FRAME CADRE SC28- 893 cm³ P.V.A. 91/6527
N° DE - Nr.
MAX. PERMISSIBLE CHARGE
POIDS TOTAL GEWICHT 392 kg
ZUL.
CYLINDREE
FZ-1
2351202

Additional security markings are always a good idea. Main purpose of this photo, though, is to show testing of side-stand safety switch. See page 75 for details

and 2001 seasons the relevant sequences became SC44A and SC44E, and then, for 2002 frames and engines, respectively, SC50A and SC50E. The 2003-model bikes were prefixed SC54A and SC54E, and then for the 2005 model year to date this became SC57A and SC57E for the frame and engine, respectively. It's also worth noting that from the 1996-season RR-T models the model year is shown (again using an industry-standard code) by means of the letter or digit immediately after each of these prefixes. Thus 'T' for 1996, 'V' for 1997, 'W' for 1998, 'X' for 1999, 'Y' for 2000, and then 1 to – so far – 8 for 2001 to 2008. (See the accompanying chart.)

The bike's official (original) colour scheme, together with its generic model designation as per the details in the paragraph immediately above this, was for a number of years recorded on a coded label on the frame below the front part of the seat. The seat is secured by two M8/13mm bolts. In later machines the colour

code is shown in the small storage compartment beneath the rear seat/tail-light unit.

Check all three items – frame number, engine number and colour code – against the information shown in the registration documents. A mismatch in either the engine number or the colour isn't necessarily particularly sinister – engines can blow up, and then are often replaced with second-hand units; enthusiastic owners quite legitimately update and customise their bikes – but obviously might require further investigation. And a discrepancy in the frame number – or any such number that looks as if it might even have been altered – should most definitely ring alarm bells.

Bear in mind that while a change of engine or colour scheme has no bearing on the bike's usability, obviously these will affect its originality. That could make it harder to sell the machine later, or perhaps worth slightly less – so either bargain accordingly, or simply take your chance and enjoy your CBR regardless.

YEAR	FRAME NUMBER PREFIX	ENGINE NUMBER PREFIX
1992 (RR-N)	SC28	SC28E-
1993 (RR-P)	SC28	SC28E-
1994 (RR-R)	SC28	SC28E-
1995 (RR-S)	SC28	SC28E-
1996 (RR-T)	SC33A-TM	SC33E-
1997 (RR-V)	SC33A-VM	SC33E-
1998 (RR-W)	SC33A-WM	SC33E-
1999 (RR-X)	SC33A-XM	SC33E-
2000 (RR-Y)	SC44A-YM	SC44E-
2001 (RR-1)	SC44A-1M	SC44E-
2002 (RR-2)	SC50A-2M	SC50E-
2003 (RR-3)	SC54A-3M	SC54E-
2004 (RR-4)	SC57A-4M	SC57E-
2005 (RR-5)	SC57A-5M	SC57E-
2006 (RR-6)	SC57A-6M	SC57E-
2007 (RR-7)	SC57A-7M	SC57E-
2008 (RR-8)	SC57A-8M	SC57E-

FireBlade colour codes

1992; RR-N

Black	NH1F
Ross White	NH196H

1993; RR-P

Black	NH1E
Ross White	NH196I

1994; RR-R

Ross White	NH196H
Sandy Beige Metallic (Urban Tiger)	YR125K
Sparkler Black Pearl (with 'CBR' decal in red)	NH343K

1995; RR-S

Ross White	NH196K
Sandy Beige Metallic (Urban Tiger)	YR125K
Sparkler Black Pearl (with 'CBR' decal in white)	NH343K

1997; RR-V

1998; RR-W

2000; RR-Y

1996; RR-T

Black	NH1B
Blitz Grey Metallic	NH254A
Sparkling Red	R127A

1997; RR-V

Black	NH1B
Pearl Citron Yellow	Y140I
Ross White	NH196K

1998; RR-W

Black	NH1D
Candy Blaze Orange	YR196D
Sparkling Red	R127H

1999; RR-X

Jerez Blue Metallic	B154B
Lapis Blue Metallic	PB257H
Sparkling Red	R127A

2000; RR-Y

Black	NH1
Sunrise Yellow	Y160
Winning Red	R258

2001; RR-1

Accurate Silver Metallic (special edition)	NH146
Italian Red	R157
Lapis Blue Metallic	PB257
Pearl Flash Yellow	Y163

2002; RR-2

Pearl Flash Yellow	Y163
Ross White	NH196
Winning Red	R258

2003; RR-3

Black	NH1B
Black and Yellow	NH1Y
Candy Tahitian Blue	PB215

2001; RR-1

2003; RR-3

2004; RR-4

2005; RR-5

2007; RR-7

2004; RR-4
Black	NH1E
Pearl Fadeless White	NH341KD
Winning Red	R258BB

2005; RR-5
Black	NH1
Candy Tahitian Blue	PB215H
Pearl Siren Blue-A (Repsol colours)	PB123
Winning Red	R258H

2006; RR-6
Graphite Black	NHB01BA

Iron Nail Silver Metallic-U	NH167EA
Winning Red	R258BA

2007; RR-7
Graphite Black	NHB01DA
Pearl Fadeless White	NH341KA
Winning Red	R258BA

2008; RR-8
Candy Glory Red
Pearl Sunbeam White
Winning Red
Graphite Black

2008; RR-8

FireBlade spotters' guide

Even the experts will readily agree that it can sometimes be extraordinarily difficult quickly to distinguish one Blade from another, unless you're lucky enough to see one from each model year parked in a long row – and sadly that doesn't happen too often.

Nevertheless, there are a number of what might be termed family features that soon help divide them into a number of

It was only the earliest bikes that had conventional round headlamps

RR-Y and later models have these so-called upside-down front forks

basic and easily identifiable groups.

The very first bikes, for instance, have two round headlights set into the rather slab-fronted fairing, and what seems by today's standards a very wide seat; you could even suggest with some justification that they look just a little old-fashioned. The fuel tank is very prominent, too, and there's a rather

ostentatious round exhaust silencer (muffler) on the right-hand side at the rear.

The first big change to the FireBlade's appearance came, as we've suggested elsewhere, in 1994, when both the characteristic fox-eye headlamps and the (optional) Urban Tiger colour schemes were introduced. In 1996 came a new twin-spar cast-aluminium frame with a so-called Yagura swinging arm, and then in 1998 both an electronic instrument panel and a distinctive tapered box-section swinging arm.

The 2000 model year saw the first use of so-called upside-down front forks and a 17-inch front wheel, and bikes from this period also have a notably squarer and rather more angular appearance than before. The right-hand side of the rear swinging arm also had what can best be termed a much more 'solid' appearance.

Two years later, for the 2002 season, the swinging arm changed yet again for the so-called Unit Pro-Link system, and quite apart from the large identifying decal proclaiming just that, now had a distinctive cut-out on its right-hand side. Meanwhile the bike itself has a much sleeker stance.

The 2004 model year brought some big and easily identified changes, too. The Unit Pro-Link swinging arm remained, much as before, but the now radially mounted front brake calipers are an immediate giveaway, and the brand-new under-seat exhaust system, together with a slimmer-looking fairing, give the bike a much more 'naked' appearance. Look out, too, for the headstock-mounted Honda Electronic Steering Damper, or HESD.

This so-called naked look was a theme that continued through 2005, 2006 and 2007, and culminated for the 2008 season with an even more vestigial fairing, a stylishly angular exhaust muffler that cleverly looks as if it's almost part of the frame, and not least a rear 'mudguard' and seat arrangement that's little more than somewhere to hang the licence plate and turn signals. It certainly doesn't look strong enough to take the weight of an adult – even though it undoubtedly is.

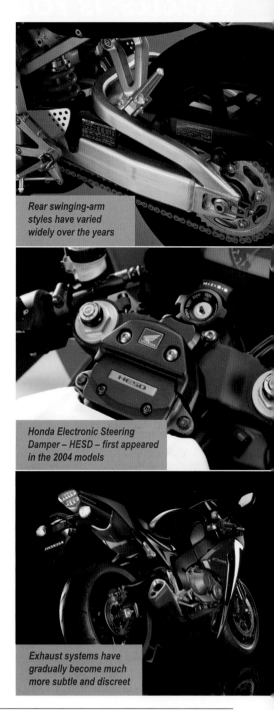

Rear swinging-arm styles have varied widely over the years

Honda Electronic Steering Damper – HESD – first appeared in the 2004 models

Exhaust systems have gradually become much more subtle and discreet

The FireBlade has been subject to a number of recalls during its now nearly 17-year production life; Honda plainly takes its responsibilities very seriously. Most of the machines on the second-hand market today will have undergone rectification work in the relevant areas, but it won't do any harm to check. Any official Honda dealership should be able to help (and also to carry out any outstanding work if necessary). Failing that, try the importer for your particular country. You will in all cases need to provide the chassis number, or Vehicle Identification Number (VIN), rather than the registration number.

In the case of the 1992 RR-N models it was possible that after repeated heavy braking from high speed one or more of the backing plates behind the front brake pads could expand because of the heat, and as a result bind against the inside of the caliper. This could prevent the affected pad(s) from returning to its/their correct rest position and thus binding against the rotor, and the resulting overheating often distorted the rotor. It would have taken the edge off the performance, too. The cure was – and remains – to fit new, later-style pads. Bikes affected were in the range SC28-2000001 to SC28-2003852, but the fact is that pads are consumable items, and you're highly unlikely today to encounter a bike still showing this specific problem.

RR-Y and RR-1 models, built during 2000 and 2001, could suffer from two known faults. In one instance the flexible feed hose from the petrol tank could be damaged internally as a result of stretching when the tank was temporarily raised for access during routine maintenance. It was considered that the subsequent potential leak posed a fire hazard, and so dealers were required to fit a longer hose.

Machines affected were in the range

SC44A3YM000001 to SC44A4YM015025, but it should be obvious whether yours still needs attention (the hose is just visible under the right-hand side of the tank). Any bike returned to an official Honda dealer for the work to be done (which, as with all such recalls, was – and is – free of charge) should have had a dot-punch mark made on the headstock next to the frame number, but obviously there's nothing to stop an unscrupulous vendor making his own mark.

The second of the RR-Y's potential faults, which it shared with the subsequent 2001-season RR-1 models, concerned the clutch and the rather alarming possibility that the rear wheel could lock. The cause was primarily the clutch judder that can occur during high-speed racing-style starts. The resulting stress could sometimes cause the clutch outer casing to fail, with pieces of metal jamming both the drive to the rear wheel and possibly even the crankshaft, both with very unpleasant consequences.

The cure involved the installation of an improved clutch casing and clutch actuating-lever shaft, together with an improved friction plate and a special anti-judder spring and spring seat. Bikes affected were in the ranges SC44AYM000294 to SC44A8YM015025 and SC44A1M103649 to SC44A1M105265, and again the rectification work was identified by a dot-punch mark, this time on the frame just above the clutch housing.

On RR-Y, RR-1, RR-2 and RR-3 models – the first to have the so-called upside-down front forks – there's also the possibility that the lower portion of either or both front fork legs could crack. This is believed to be caused by water and road salt finding their way down between the outer casting and the main tube and corroding the aluminium, thus forcing the two components apart. The cure – actually,

it's a preventive measure; cracked components must always be replaced – is simply to run a bead of silicone sealant round the affected joint. Bikes affected were in the range JH2SDC44AYM000294–YM013050 (RR-Y), 1M103649–1M106961 (RR-1), 2M001433–2M009728 (RR-2) and finally 3M100041–3M107921 (RR-3 models).

More recently Honda recalled a small number of 2004-model machines to fix a potential fault in the by now digital speedometer that could suggest that the machine was travelling up to 25 per cent more slowly than it actually was. An indicated 50mph (80kph), in other words, could in point of fact be as much as 62mph (99kph), with obvious ramifications as far as the owner's already possibly less than perfect driving history is concerned.

The simple way to check whether the work has been done – or if it's required – is to ride at precisely 2000rpm in second gear. If the speedo is accurate it should read exactly 18mph (29–30kph). Anything less than that and the problem remains to be sorted. Bikes affected were in the range JH2SC57A04M000001 to JH2SC57A04M009594. Bear in mind here that although the odometer (distance recorder) wasn't affected,

the new speedometer probably won't have been reset to reflect the bike's mileage at the time of the change, and so could now be under-reading by several thousand miles or more.

There have also been several 'product updates' during the CBR's production life. Essentially this was work that would have been carried out – again free of charge – if the owner complained of a specific problem. Some RR-2s, for instance, suffered from vibration in the steering-head bearings, in which case dealers were instructed to remove the original taper-roller bearings and fit the later bikes' needle-roller items. Bikes potentially affected here were in the range JH2SC50A*2M000001 to JH2SC50A*2M009833, and again the work will have been identified with a dot-punch mark on the headstock next to the frame number.

Still other RR-2s had – or may still have – what's known as a waisted support strap round the silencer (muffler) can, rather than the later type that's the same full width all the way round. These straps can break, and the resulting stress on the silencer can fracture that. Bikes affected were in the range JH2SC50A*2M000001 to JH2SC50A*2M006683 – obviously putting some of them in the same group as for the steering-head update.

What to take with you

A wheeled service jack (known as a trolley jack in the UK) isn't perhaps the most obviously useful piece of equipment to take with you when inspecting a motorcycle with a view to buying it, but it's well worth considering none the less.

To inspect (and subsequently to adjust) the drive chain properly it's helpful to be able to rotate the rear wheel freely, and assessing the condition of the no less crucial steering-head bearings ideally means lifting the front wheel well clear of the ground, too. In both cases this also makes inspection of the brakes easier. And since the Blade has only a side-stand this can be quite tricky without a jack.

You have to be careful how you use it, though. Honda concedes that a Blade can safely be lifted from beneath the engine (which assumes the exhaust system and in later bikes the fairing has been removed), but in practice it's absolutely essential to spread the load against the underside of the four relatively fragile exhaust pipes with a block of wood. And you will definitely need an assistant to steady the bike while it's up in the air, even if it's only an inch or two. Don't be tempted to rely on its inherent balance, or you could end up with a nasty and possibly very painful and expensive surprise.

A far better alternative – at least for inspecting and later servicing the rear end – is a so-called paddock stand. This is no more than a tubular-steel frame – usually adjustable, and so suitable for different bikes – which slides under both sides of the swinging arm. Bikes built from 2002 on have paddock-stand 'bobbins' – or locating lugs – on the swinging arm. Likewise after-market so-called 'crash buttons' at the base of the front forks, designed to protect these highly vulnerable castings in the event of even a minor accident, also make a very useful mounting point for a paddock stand.

Pull the stand backwards so that it pivots on its wheels, and it will then safely hold the bike upright, with the latter's rear wheel a couple of inches off the ground. You might find the bike's current owner has one already, but if you're serious about owning a FireBlade it would be worth either borrowing or buying one even before you start. They're not expensive.

As far as other inspection equipment is concerned, you can be either as thorough or as minimalist as you choose. A good, bright torch is always useful and, since you could be crawling around on the ground, so might be a pair of coveralls and/or something soft to lie on. Likewise, you could take a pair of latex gloves to avoid having to wash your hands after checking the drive chain and various other greasy bits. Beyond that, though, you're into the realms of the more specialised inspection – cylinder-compression testers, micrometers and so on – that by definition means you probably won't need this book to tell you what to do.

The ideal way of getting either the front or the rear wheel clear of the ground for inspection is by means of a so-called paddock stand like this

Engine

The FireBlade's power unit and transmission are built up as a single compact assembly, with all of the major external components and casings made from a lightweight aluminium (or occasionally magnesium) alloy. There are inevitably a great many detail differences between early and late units, which limits the interchangeability of parts, but essentially they're all the same basic design.

The engine is a liquid-cooled in-line four, mounted transversely across the frame – the cylinders are numbered from one to four from the left as you're sitting astride the bike – and like most of its type has a horizontally split crankcase. The crankshaft runs in conventional shell-type bearings, with similar items for the connecting-rods. The pressure-fed lubrication system is of the wet-sump type (there's no separate oil-storage tank, in other words), with a chain-driven, twin-rotor pump. The sump pan, at the lowest part of the crankcase, is removable separately, and sealed with a gasket. There's also an external oil-to-water oil-cooler, mounted on the front of the engine behind the oil filter, which is itself located within the arc formed by the four-branch exhaust manifold.

Each cylinder has two inlet and two exhaust valves, each of those pairs actuated by one of two overhead camshafts, themselves driven by a single, internally toothed chain from a sprocket at the right-hand end of the crankshaft. The inlet camshaft is at the rear of the engine, the exhaust camshaft at the front. Valve-clearance adjustment – which should be checked and if necessary adjusted every 16,000 miles or two years, whichever is the sooner – is by means of replaceable shims. Unlike many of Honda's later bikes, such as the VFR range of machines, the FireBlade has no form of variable valve timing, even in its most recent form.

All engines are DOHC water-cooled fours, mounted transversely

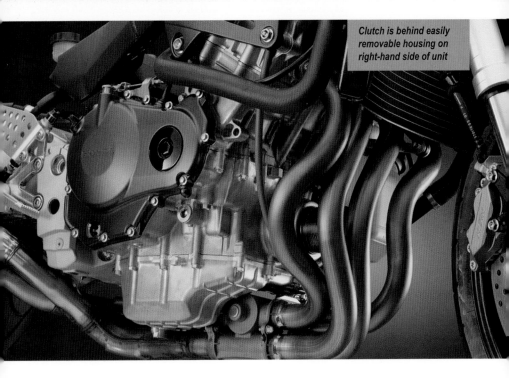

Clutch is behind easily removable housing on right-hand side of unit

The alternator is mounted at the left-hand end of the crankshaft, with a one-way clutch for the starter motor incorporated into the outer part of the alternator rotor. The coolant pump, too, is mounted on the left-hand side of the engine, and is driven by means of the oil-pump shaft. (The radiator, naturally enough, is up front, inside the fairing just below the steering head.)

The engine is a robust, reliable and remarkably long-lasting piece of machinery, and most, if not all, of the few problems you might encounter will probably be the result of deliberate misuse and/or neglect, signs of which should generally be easy to spot. The former is most likely to include persistent use of very high revs (particularly damaging if the oil and coolant aren't at the correct operating temperature, or are of the wrong type). Over-revving can also take its toll, particularly if the transmission has started to wear (see below) and as a result

occasionally to jump out of gear.

Check the service history for evidence that the oil and filter have been changed at the correct intervals. Honda stipulates every 8000 miles or 12 months, but most experts agree that 4000 miles or six months is safer, and not a lot more costly in view of the longevity benefits it generally brings. You need only four litres of oil for a full change; that's considerably less than in a comparable sports car. Note, too, that it's vitally important to use oil of the correct type and grade. Honda recommends a good-quality SF- or SG-grade SAE 10W40-viscosity mineral or semi-synthetic – but not a fully synthetic product. As a 5/40 that would be too thin, and could possibly lead to problems such as clutch slip (it's a so-called 'wet' clutch) and even overheating.

In order to check the level and condition of the engine oil in your intended purchase, first let the motor run for a few minutes to warm it up (better

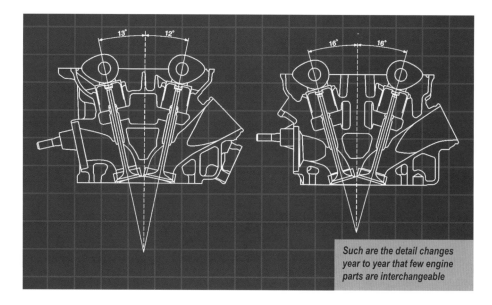

Such are the detail changes year to year that few engine parts are interchangeable

still, take the bike for a short test-run, or have the owner do so) and let it stand at rest for two or three minutes for the circulating oil to drain back down into the sump. If you don't do this you could get a misleadingly low reading.

Pre-1995 models have a filler cap/dipstick on the right-hand crankcase cover. With the bike held fully upright wipe any dirt from the cap, unscrew it, and then replace it lightly in the orifice, but without actually screwing it back in. The oil should be somewhere between the upper and lower marks on the dipstick (and ideally nearer the upper mark).

The 1995 and later models have a sight glass in the bottom of the clutch cover,

again on the right-hand side of the bike (and with the filler cap at the top of the clutch cover). With the bike again held in an upright position, check that the oil is somewhere between the two marks provided. In both cases the oil should be light brown to dark brown in colour, with no obvious particles floating around in it. It certainly shouldn't be black and/or smell burned.

The engine should start instantly on the button (there's no kick-starter), whether hot or cold (pre-2000 bikes with carburettors have a cable-operated choke control on the handlebars), and quickly settle down to a smooth, even idle at around 1100–1200rpm depending on specification and the market the bike was sold in. US-market models generally tend to idle just a little faster than European ones.

The engine speed should remain constant as you push the handlebars slowly from one lock stop to the other, and also when you pull in the clutch lever. If it rises or possibly even falls suspect

Valve-clearance adjustment is by means of fiddly but reliable shims

poorly routed throttle and/or choke cables or, more seriously in the case of the clutch lever, that there's excessive lateral movement in the crankshaft, or some other internal problem that will need further investigation.

Starter motors aren't known for any particular problems – but be suspicious none the less if it's unduly noisy or lazy. (Although that might be nothing more than a tired battery; see the section on the electrical system). There's no oil-pressure gauge, as such, but the red warning light in the instrument panel should come on when the main ignition switch is actuated, and then go out again just a few seconds – at the very latest – after the engine has fired.

Beware the absence of said warning light (the bulb may have blown, but then again someone may have removed it deliberately in order to mask any problems), and likewise be suspicious if it comes on at any time when the engine is running. The sender unit may be faulty, but equally there may be a problem with either the lubrication system (have it checked by a dealer or some other specialist with an accurate external pressure gauge) or the crankshaft and/or the connecting-rod bearings.

You can sometimes confirm the latter by the presence of either a heavy rumbling sound (crankshaft bearings) or a knock under load (con-rods). The factory's specified oil pressure is 70psi (4.9 bar) at 6000rpm with the oil temperature at 80 degrees Celsius. The oil pick-up pipe is at the front end of the sump, and so can be starved of crucial lubricant during prolonged wheelies, or even just very hard acceleration. Obviously this will be a particular problem if there is less than the required amount of oil in the system to start with.

Look for any obvious oil and/or coolant leaks from joint faces and pipe connections (there shouldn't be any; this is a Honda we're talking about!), and carefully examine the various

Special cutaway display engine shows just how complex Blade really is

Crankcase has car-type bolt-on sump, plus spin-on oil-filter element

Later fuel injection very rarely requires attention. But carbs reliable, too

casings and their fixing screws for signs of less than expert attention. And don't forget the underside of the power unit: the removable sump plate is prone to damage and subsequent leaks as a result of the careless use of a workshop jack or hitting kerbs, and raising the bike in this way might also cause problems with the exhaust system and/or fairing.

Make sure the crankcase drain plug (accessible from the left-hand side of the bike once the fairing has been removed, almost directly under the gear-change shaft) hasn't been butchered, and try to establish if a new sealing washer was used when it was last refitted. Beware, too, of after-market so-called 'crash buttons', bolted through the frame into either side of the cylinder head. It's not uncommon to find that their fixing bolts have been drastically over-tightened, damaging the holes in the head casting to such an extent that the only effective cure is to have a specialist engineering shop fit threaded inserts.

Such is the design of the valvegear that tappet noise is unlikely (the clearances tend to close up in service rather than expand), but it's worth listening for the heavier knocking (at half engine speed) that could suggest worn camshaft lobes or followers. Certainly this is rare, but not impossible, particularly if the bike has run extended oil-change intervals. Some owners suggest that its automatic adjuster can allow the camshaft chain to rattle rather noisily at idle, particularly in the 929cc and 954cc engines, and that it's best replaced by a manual device, but still others (main dealers included) will tell you that they've never had a problem. Either way, listen for that tell-tale rattle.

A compression check, should you wish to carry one out, should give you readings of around 170psi, or about 12.0 bar. This is a fairly involved task and, assuming the vendor agrees, you should remember that any checks that

involve you taking the bike apart could expose you to liabilities resulting from component failures later, should you not buy it. If in doubt, have any 'invasive' checks performed by an expert. It's also not as easy to get at the spark plugs on later bikes as it is in the earlier ones.

Experience is the best guide as to what is an acceptable variation in compression readings and what isn't (which again makes it a job for a specialist if you don't have such knowledge yourself), but be suspicious if any cylinder is more than 10–15 per cent down compared to its neighbours. Isolate valve and valve-seat problems from cylinder-bore and/or piston-ring wear by squirting engine oil into the cylinders. If it's the valves, any subsequent reading will tend to remain the same; if it's the rings or bores it will possibly increase. Alternatively – and this is an even more complex task, and one that demands complete co-operation from the vendor – consider having what's known as a cylinder-leakage test carried out.

The cooling system has no particular vices – and none that you won't find in any other liquid-cooled engine. Remember, though, that the all-alloy construction of the motor makes it absolutely essential that the coolant is a 50/50 per cent mix of water (ideally distilled) and corrosion-inhibiting ethylene glycol-based anti-freeze throughout the year, and never just plain tap water. Such is the penetrating nature of anti-freeze, though, that this does at least make it easy to spot leaks. Look for tell-tale green or blue stains. You should never use any form of leak-sealing compound, says Honda.

As a would-be buyer just about the only obvious and easy check you can carry out on the coolant is to hold the bike upright on flat ground and make sure that the level in the translucent plastic coolant reservoir is somewhere between the upper and lower marks (and, as with the engine oil, ideally nearer the

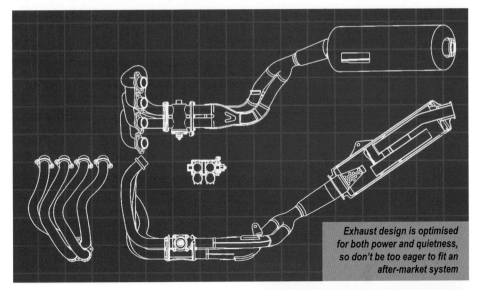

Exhaust design is optimised for both power and quietness, so don't be too eager to fit an after-market system

upper one). The motor should be at its normal operating temperature for this, but if possible it's worth a quick look – just in case – before either you or the vendor fires it up from cold. Better that than a cooked engine.

Other than that, check that the external rubber pipes and their worm-drive clips are in reasonable condition (and of the correct type and material, rather than odd bits of generic hose), check the radiator for signs of stone or other impact damage, and make sure that the temperature gauge (a digital unit after 1997) does at least appear to be working correctly. With the engine hot after a run it should read around 80 degrees (the sender unit is located under the fuel tank). The electric fan should come on automatically when the gauge reaches around 90 degrees, and switch itself off again when it drops back to about 75-80 degrees. If the fan fails to respond, then the most likely culprit will be the thermostatic switch at the left-hand side of the radiator, although such is the exposed position of the fan that the motor and/or its shaft may have seized.

Choke control is self-explanatory, but naturally fitted only to bikes with carburettors. Check all cooling-system connections for leaks (below)

Transmission

The clutch, which is gear-driven from the right-hand end of the crankshaft, is of the wet, multi-plate type.

All Honda FireBlades have a six-speed, constant-mesh gearbox. The shift pattern is shown for reference on the drive-sprocket cover – so you can see it only by climbing off the bike – but is of the familiar one-down-five-up pattern, with neutral located between first and second.

The clutch should feel both light and progressive, with a smooth, linear action from the handlebar lever. Check the cable first (where relevant) if it's stiff or jerky. As with the throttle cable (see the Engine section), it may be poorly routed, kinked or damaged, but then again it might just need some lubrication through a pressurised cable oiler. From the 2004 model year the release mechanism is actuated hydraulically, and any roughness in the lever's movement will more likely be the result of some internal clutch problem.

In all cases watch out for the juddering as you pull away from rest that might indicate burned friction plates or damaged clutch drums (and see also the earlier section on recalls for details that affected certain bikes). Test for signs of slipping by selecting fifth or sixth gear and then

Chain and sprockets need to be examined very closely for wear

accelerating reasonably hard from about 40–50mph. There should be an obvious and direct correlation between engine speed and road speed.

Check the clutch switch – designed to prevent the engine being started with the transmission in gear unless the clutch lever is also pulled in – by sitting on the bike and attempting to do just that. The switch itself, if you should ever need to replace it, is situated within the clutch lever's mounting bracket on the handlebars.

Clutch drag – when the plates don't separate fully, and when gear selection, particularly into first when you're at a standstill, is either noisy or notchy – might be caused by nothing more serious than poor cable adjustment or a stretched cable. The solution is obvious (there's an adjustment point at each end of the cable) but don't discount the possibility of

the previously mentioned damaged clutch drums. In later bikes with a hydraulic clutch the problem may be either leaking seals or (usually as a direct result of those leaky seals, of course) a low fluid level in the reservoir. Clutches can rattle annoyingly, too, but this is rarely serious.

Either way, the good news is that renewing the complete clutch is by no means the complicated and expensive job it might well be in a car, especially one with this level of performance. The task can be done in its entirety in little more than a couple of hours, and with only fairly basic tools. You certainly shouldn't let suspected clutch problems alone put you off an otherwise sound bike.

Gearboxes are generally no less reliable – and that in spite of the huge power they have to cope with, and sometimes the remarkably heavy-handed riders, too.

Engine number should be clearly visible just in-board of clutch housing

Few engines will still be as clean as this, but major oil leaks are rare

(And don't forget that they have to share their lubricating oil with the invariably hard-working engine.) That said, over-frequent wheelies, and crashed or even missed gear changes, are inevitably going to take their toll on something sooner or later, and you might well find that your prospective bike jumps out of third and fourth gear (and sometimes second, as well).

This usually happens under power rather than on the over-run (which, as you'll imagine, can rather take the wind out of your sails). It's usually the result of bent selector forks and/or worn actuating grooves in the selector drum that pushes the forks into the required positions as you move the gear-change lever with your foot. It's not impossible for individual gears to become chipped, or to lose complete teeth, but a bike with problems this serious will probably (and very visibly) be on its last legs in just about every other respect. Transmission bearings rarely become noisy unless the oil has been neglected, and are not too difficult to replace, but under these circumstances the engine will usually let go first.

Fuel and exhaust systems

The FireBlade's fuel and exhaust systems are in principle very simple (and also remarkably similar from 1992 right the way through to the present day), and should hold no great terrors for would-be buyers.

The nominally 17- to 18-litre (4.8 US gallon) steel tank is mounted via shock-absorbing rubber blocks on the frame immediately above the engine, and is secured by a single bolt at each end (although 1996 models have two bolts at the front). Shake the tank gently from side to side to establish that it's securely attached to the frame, but at the same time retains the small amount of movement permitted by the rubber damping blocks.

Any damage to the tank will usually be obvious enough, but it's worth checking very carefully none the less. It's a large and important part of the machine's visual appeal, and while some wear and tear at the rear end is inevitable – if only from the rider's knees rubbing against it – deeper scratches and definitely any dents are best avoided (or the bike's price adjusted downward accordingly). Check for leaks, too, and for the same reason you should ideally have the vendor fill the tank as close to the brim as possible before making your final decision. You can always pay the

Fuel tank is carefully moulded to make best use of limited space

extra for the fuel needed if this is necessary.

All bikes have a locking filler cap with a fold-flat release blade. The cap, too, should be leak-free, and the blade both easy to turn and fold. Devoid of a car-style catalytic converter until the 2007 model year, all but the most recent Blades can generally run on either unleaded fuel or, in the now few places where it's still available (and legal), good, old-fashioned leaded. Or a mixture of both. Either way, the minimum usable grade is 91 RON, but it's worth using 97-octane even if it's more expensive than the regular grade.

In earlier bikes (RR-N to RR-X models) fuel flow from the tank is controlled by a gravity-fed tap, which also allows access to a reserve supply of around 3.5 litres (0.9 US gallons).

The latter should be sufficient for around 20 miles (32km) at normal road speeds, and a bit more than that if you take it easy. These machines also have a relay-controlled electric fuel pump mounted under the tank, and again for safety reasons designed to work only when the engine is actually running. For cold-starting there is a simple cable-operated choke control on the steering head.

RR-T to RR-Y models have a vacuum-operated fuel tap (with approximately the same 3.5-litre/20-mile reserve supply), but neither an electric pump nor a choke control. Again this set-up will cut the fuel to the engine as soon as the latter stops running. Cold-start fuelling is in this case handled by a throttle sensor mounted

Exposed early-type exhaust must be securely attached for safety

Don't forget to check for obvious dangers such as a leaking fuel filler

on the carburettors and connected to the ignition control unit. In all cases carburation itself is either by means of four 38mm (1.5in) constant-vacuum Keihin carburettors (RR-N to RR-X models) or, in the case of 2000-model RR-Y and all subsequent bikes, a combined electronic fuel-injection and ignition system of, as you would expect, gradually increasing sophistication, complexity and efficiency.

The only pre-purchase checks you can realistically carry out are to the condition of the various rubber hoses beneath the tank (and see also the Recalls section to find out more about the safety check applicable to the main fuel hose on certain models). Other potential sources of fuel leaks – usually evidenced by tell-tale staining and/or a smell of fuel – include the various gaskets and rubber 'O'-rings in both the carburettors and the fuel tap, but all of the parts you might need to cure them are available from Honda dealers, and reasonably cheap.

The work isn't particularly difficult, either.

Carburettor problems, as such, are fairly rare. (And the later injection system is reliable enough that you can simply forget about it.) Worn throttle spindles cause air leaks that might lead to poor running (and particularly to a poor tickover; the engine should idle smoothly and evenly at around 900rpm when hot), but this is usually only in bikes that have covered a huge mileage. A more likely cause of rough idling is either poorly synchronised carburettors (a specialist job to check, and certainly to rectify) or else split rubber diaphragms inside the units' vacuum chambers (which, with a degree of DIY skill, you can put right yourself). Failure of the diaphragms will also cause hesitation under acceleration. You might also (eventually) discover that one or more of the float chambers has the wrong fuel level in it, but this too is unlikely unless someone who can't resist uninformed tinkering has owned the bike.

Earlier carb-fed bikes have the convenience of a fast-idle control

That said, it's worth checking the two throttle cables both for the required freedom of movement and the small but equally essential free play they must incorporate. Indeed, Honda recommends that this should be done every 8000 miles (12,000km) or 12 months in any case. With the engine switched off make sure first that the throttle twistgrip rotates smoothly and easily from fully closed to fully open and back again, and will also quickly and automatically snap back to fully closed whenever you release it. This is an important safety feature. Repeat the test with the steering turned to various different angles, and not least at full left- and right-hand locks. Now start the engine and ensure that rotating the steering head makes no appreciable difference to the idle speed. Check also that the inner end of the twistgrip will move between 2.0–6.0mm (0.1–0.25in) – measured between its inner flange and the handlebar switch housing

– before you hear the engine begin to speed up.

It's much the same procedure for the choke cable – where fitted. With the engine switched off, pull the knob on the handlebars up to the full-on position, and then push it back in again. The movement should be smooth and free, with the knob locking securely into position at any desired point, and the linkage on the carburettors – visible from the right-hand side of the bike – extending fully and then retracting again. In this case there's no specific figure for the necessary free play in the system, other than that the choke mechanism must genuinely be fully off whenever the knob is pushed fully home.

In both cases stiffness may be caused either by seized and/or poorly routed cables (lubrication and/or repositioning might help, unless they've been damaged by their ordeal), or else problems within the carburettor/choke linkage itself. Even that, though, is unlikely to be something you couldn't cure by lubrication alone, or failing that by careful dismantling and reassembly.

As far as the exhaust is concerned, start by making sure that it's actually legal. This is unlikely to be an issue if it's the genuine Honda or a reputable after-market system – unless there's something wrong with it, of course – but some poorer-quality 'performance' silencers do precious little in the way of quietening the engine, and could even land you in trouble with the law. They might also result in you being turned away from some trackdays – with no refund – where a noise limit is enforced. If in doubt seek professional advice – and don't simply rely on the word of the vendor.

Problems, as such, are again rare, and usually easily solved. Older and poorly maintained bikes might be suffering from blowing joints here and there, especially where the four-branch manifold (header) meets the

cylinder head, but it's usually straightforward enough to fit new sealing rings – provided you can undo the eight securing nuts, of course. See also the warning about the so-called waisted silencer support in the Recalls section.

Later standard bikes – from the 2000-model RR-Y onward – have the added sophistication of a motor-driven valve in the exhaust, and this, mounted over the rear wheel (or in the end can from the RR-4 onward), can occasionally cause problems. It was designed to offer more torque at low to medium engine speeds, but like any such mechanism it requires occasional cleaning and lubrication. If this isn't done it can seize up and then burn out the electric motor, which will in turn activate the fuel-injection warning light on the instrument panel (and also generate a fault code within the engine management system). Obviously there's no point at all fitting a new motor without first freeing off the mechanism.

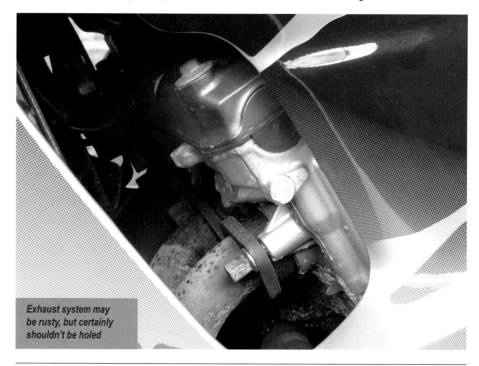

Exhaust system may be rusty, but certainly shouldn't be holed

Final drive: chain and sprockets

Hub has shock-damping rubber coupling: check for signs of deterioration

As with the CBR's brakes (see the next section), so it is for what's known as the final drive – the chain and its two sprockets, which between them also determine the bike's overall gearing. Problems in this area are both relatively rare and, when they do occur, fairly easy to spot and then rectify.

With a minimum of 124bhp (91kW) – and as much as 180bhp (132kW) – passing through the chain, itself often sprayed with muddy or salty water, it's no surprise that it

needs to be checked – and, if necessary, to have its tension adjusted – every 500–600 miles. Indeed, at sustained high speeds, or under particularly fierce acceleration – after a trackday, for instance, or if you're in the habit of pulling wheelies – it may even need to be checked and adjusted more frequently than this.

To do this, first park the bike on its side-stand (or have an assistant hold it upright on its wheels) and, with the engine switched off, select neutral. Now with your hand (use latex gloves to keep yourself clean) check the slack in the lower run of the chain, midway between the two sprockets. It should be free to move up and down 25 to 35mm (an inch to an inch and a half). More than 50mm (two inches) of slack can cause the chain to damage the swinging arm. An index mark on the left-hand chain adjuster will indicate when it has become dangerously stretched.

Roll the bike forward a few feet (or rotate the rear wheel if it's clear of the ground) and recheck the slack, and repeat the same process several more times. The slack should remain constant. If it doesn't, the chances are that a number of links in the chain are binding or even semi-permanently kinked. Often this can be temporarily fixed, if not eliminated, by removing the chain and cleaning it, and

then soaking it in a bath of special grease. But clearly it's a bargaining point – and possibly an indication of how well the bike has been maintained. Either way, a chain in this condition is well past its best, and should be replaced as soon as possible.

You can check the chain further, even while it's on the bike, by slowly rotating the rear wheel and inspecting it literally inch by inch: it should take only a minute or two. Look for damaged rollers and loose pins, as well as dry or rusted links and, if you've keen eyes, missing 'O'-ring seals. These can be damaged by steam cleaning, pressure washing and also some chemicals. The chain should be cleaned using only a high-flashpoint solvent such as paraffin, and even then you should soak it for no more than a few minutes. Any problems that can't be

Ideally the chain needs a link-by-link inspection. Check teeth for hooking

solved by lubrication alone will again require the chain to be renewed without question.

Look out for the chain's joining or so-called master link – which will either have recognisable identification marks or may even be a completely different colour to its neighbours. This must be of the fully staked type rather than the old-fashioned sort with a simple 'U'-shaped clip. You should also check for evidence of poor installation (which, like 'breaking' the chain, can be done only with a special tool). Cracking of the side plate(s) and damaged 'O'-rings are the usual giveaways.

The sprocket on the rear wheel is easy to examine, but the one at the gearbox end is behind an aluminium cover that will have to be removed. This will also allow you to inspect the drive-chain guide plate, or 'slider', designed to protect the swinging arm from the chain, and which will require replacement if worn beyond the line marked on its surface. The most likely sprocket problems are hooked teeth caused by wear on their working faces, in which case you'll have to budget for a pair of new ones – and a new chain, too, since that will almost certainly have been damaged by the incorrect profile of the teeth. Conversely, whenever you fit a new chain you'll also have to fit a pair of new sprockets, too. They're not massively expensive, though.

The only other area you might need to check – but this depends to a large extent on the bike's general presentation – is the rubber drive coupling inside the rear wheel hub. This is designed to offer a degree of shock absorbency, and naturally leads almost as hard a life as the chain. If severely abused or otherwise damaged it will make its presence known by spitting out flecks of rubber – trackday CBRs famously suffer

Chain adjustment easy enough, but it's vital to ensure both sides of wheel spindle are moved by the same amount to preserve correct alignment

markedly from this – and you'll probably feel its absence as a surging or harshness when you ride the bike on smaller throttle openings. Otherwise a degree of dismantling is required to inspect and replace it, so you might want to leave that until you've bought the bike. Again, though, the work is neither difficult nor hugely expensive.

Finally, remember that while the calibrated marks on both sides of the swinging arm are a useful guide to adjusting the chain, and at the same time preserving the correct wheel alignment, they're not infallible. It's possible, in other words, that by relying on them alone you'll end up with the rear wheel slightly out of line with the front, with all sorts of strange and possibly unpleasant effects on the handling. If you're in any doubt check it with a known straight edge.

Brakes

t's usually obvious if a CBR's brakes need attention – even before you ride it. The three large-diameter but none the less surprisingly thin rotors are right out in the open for all to see, and it's only a little more difficult to check the thickness of the equally important friction pads.

Ideally the rotors – two at the front, and one at the rear on the right-hand side – should be uniformly silver-coloured on both sides, with no sign of either rust or the characteristic blueing that comes from overheating. Look for radial cracks, particularly around the cross-drillings, as well as for deep scoring – although some marking is inevitable – and general wear and tear. Make sure the rotors are the right way round. They should be marked with an arrow pointing in the normal direction of travel.

Check, too, that the rotors are securely fixed

Bikes to end of 2003 year had Nissin calipers, then Tokico; note different attachment points. Wheel-spindle housings can crack where they meet forks

to the wheel hubs (but don't burn your fingers; if the bike has just been ridden, even if only gently, they'll probably be very hot). Standard (early) rotors are rigidly bolted to the hub, but some after-market items (and later standard ones) are fully floating units. That's to say they're attached to a carrier that, in an attempt to reduce the judder that might result from slight misalignment, allows the disc a degree of lateral movement.

Discs should obviously not be badly worn or scored, but are easy and cheap enough to renew if they are. Check carefully for slightest fluid leaks

The rotors' nominal thickness (and their diameter) varies from year to year (and from make to make in the case of after-market items), but in all cases a pronounced ridge round the circumference of either friction face will give you a quick and useful guide as to how much metal has been ground away by the pads. Most rotors (and certainly all original-equipment items) are stamped with their minimum thickness; check them with a micrometer if necessary. Renew front rotors only as a pair, never singly.

Layout of the braking system is such that fluid leaks will generally be very obvious. Make sure all mountings and pipe connections are secure

The pads should be renewed, again as a wheel set at the front, with either standard Honda items or else the uprated material of your choice, when they're down to around 4.0mm thick. Original-equipment Honda pads have wear-indicator grooves. When these disappear the pads should be replaced. Remember, though, that 'harder' pads, while better able to withstand heavy use, won't necessarily offer quite the same quick response as the standard friction material until they're good and hot.

There are essentially two types of caliper. Earlier bikes (to the end of the 2003 model year) have Nissin units, with side-facing mounting bolts on the front forks, but on 2004 and later machines the calipers are by Tokico, and mounted on the forks by means of rear-facing bolts. Later still, and reflecting the fact that the front rotors had by then been slightly enlarged, the Tokico calipers have roughly 5.0mm-thick aluminium spacers between them and their mountings.

The hydraulic system is generally no less trouble-free than any other part of the bike. Pull hard on the brake lever and simultaneously firmly press the brake pedal for a few seconds to check for signs of fluid leaks and ballooning in the flexible rubber hoses (two at the front, one at the rear). Make sure the brake light comes on when either circuit is activated. The rear switch is adjustable, but the one at the front must be renewed if it doesn't work reliably.

Check, too, that all of the hoses are not only in good condition, with no cracks or splits in the rubber, but are also correctly routed and securely attached to the forks and swinging arm (by means of proper rubber-lined 'P'-clips, basically, and not just cable-ties). This is particularly important where an owner has installed after-market braided lines (claimed to resist ballooning better, and thus to offer a more solid feel to the lever and pedal), and might not have attached them in quite the way Honda intended. Braided hoses are also more difficult to check for splits and perishing; renew them as a matter of routine if you buy the bike and suspect they may be more than a couple of years old.

Ingeniously, all of the calipers, and various other points around the bike, feature cast lugs designed to prevent the 'banjo' fittings on the flexible hoses rotating out of alignment as you tighten their central fixing bolts, and thus stretching the hoses. Make sure the lugs are present and correct, and obviously that the hoses are correctly routed round them.

It's plainly worth checking both the level and condition of the brake fluid. In truth there's not much you can do about the latter other than to change it (Honda recommends every 12,000 miles, 20,000km or 18 months). You can assess the former by holding the bike upright and looking first at the translucent plastic reservoir on the right-hand handlebar (for the front brakes), and then at the similar container (for the rear brake) just inside the frame immediately behind and below the right-hand rear corner of the fuel tank. (The fluid tank is outside on the rear part of the frame on later bikes.) The level will drop as the pads wear – and, conversely, pushing the pistons even a little way back into their bores in order to fit new pads will inevitably raise the level again, and might even cause either reservoir to overflow if it has previously been topped up.

Honda's own maintenance schedule makes no recommendations on the matter, but common sense suggests that the hydraulic seals throughout the braking system (master cylinders and calipers, in other words) should also be replaced every 12,000 miles, 20,000km or 18 months, although you could probably push that to two years quite safely. Check the invoices that come with the bike to see whether this has been carried out, and if not then budget

to do it (or to have it done for you) as soon as possible. This – or even simply a pad change – will also provide the opportunity to check the light-alloy calipers for the corrosion that can sometimes cause the pads to bind, and thus not to retract correctly from the discs. Normally this corrosion can be scraped off and the calipers rebuilt, but in severe cases you may need to fit complete new units – which obviously might also be a good opportunity to upgrade.

One final point worth noting is that the front brake lever can quite easily be adjusted to cater for those with smaller hands by bringing its outer end closer to the handlebars – but without, of course, affecting either the adjustment or the efficiency of the system itself. Simply turn the knurled wheel at the inner end of the lever – there's a click-stop detent every 90 degrees – to achieve the desired result.

Front brake lever has an ingenious mechanism to allow adjustment for riders with smaller hands. Check level of fluid in hydraulic reservoir(s)

Wheels and tyres

All CBRs come – or originally came, anyway – as standard with cast aluminium-alloy wheels designed to accept tubeless tyres – and tubeless tyres only, note. Pre-2000 bikes have a 17-inch-diameter rear wheel and a 16-inch-diameter front wheel – which famously contributed to their breathtaking agility through corners, but which also made the entire front end much more twitchy. Later machines (from the RR-Y onwards, in other words) have 17-inch wheels both front and rear. This switch also marked the change to the so-called upside-down front forks.

It's theoretically possible, by the way, to replace an earlier 16-inch front wheel with the 17-inch rim from various other contemporary Hondas (albeit in conjunction with a number of other smaller components), and today this will give you access to a wider range of tyres. If your prospective bike has been thus converted make sure the work has been done properly. Be aware, too, that until the end of the 1999 model year both front and rear wheels had six spokes apiece, but from the start of the 2000 season just three.

Specific wheel-and-tyre problems are rare – beyond the CBR range's fairly well-known appetite for wheel bearings, particularly at the rear; try to use only Honda parts for longevity – but it's sensible to carry out some basic checks. The most obvious – and particularly if you feel any untoward vibration during your test-ride – is to make sure that the wheels are actually

Raising front wheel like this allows you fully to check tyre – and forks

Rear tyres are one of the FireBlade's most obvious 'consumables'

Wheels (and brake rotors) should be marked with a directional arrow like this

round and running true.

In its simplest sense this means raising each rim clear of the ground by means of your jack and/or paddock stand, and then spinning it by hand (which should also highlight any problems of the brake pads binding, or visibly distorted rotors/discs). Any significant deviation – either up and down, or else from side to side – should be fairly obvious, and even more so if you make up a simple pointer from a piece of wire bent to shape and taped to the nearest fork or swinging-arm member.

Have a good look, too, for cracks and flat spots on the wheels, and for dents, either inward- or outward-facing, where the

bead of the tyre touches the rim. Damage here is a common cause of slow air leaks. Be suspicious of large numbers of (stick-on) balance weights that may suggest someone has tried to mask any distortion. Listen and feel for wheel-bearing problems – a rumbling noise as you spin the wheel, or perhaps tight spots, although this may be masked by the slight drag of the pads – and double-check by grasping each rim at two points roughly opposite each other and attempting to rock it on its spindle.

It's highly unlikely to be an issue, but make sure that both wheels are fitted the right way round in either the forks or the swinging arm. (You never know...) As with

Earlier machines have a 16-inch front wheel and specially designed tyre...

...but from the 2000 season conventional 17-inch items were fitted

the brake discs, an arrow cast into the spokes identifies the normal direction of travel. And, as with the power unit, look for signs of obviously chewed-up screw or bolt heads on any relevant fixings that could suggest a rather haphazard approach to servicing and repairs.

Wheel alignment is less easy to check, but again worth the effort if you're keen on the bike but suspect there may be a hidden frame problem leading to odd handling traits. It's possible to do it yourself with a tape measure and a known straight edge such as a piece of wood – or even a length of string – but most motorcycle dealers or repair shops ought to be able to oblige for

a modest cost. Don't forget to check both wheels in both planes – that the rear wheel tracks exactly behind the front, in other words – and also that both wheels are mounted true in their forks.

Tyres should obviously be of a known and reputable brand – Honda fits Bridgestone, Michelin and Pirelli as original equipment – and marked with the correct speed rating – in this case 'Z'-rated for speeds over 150mph. Make sure they're both fitted the right way round, too. As with the wheels and discs, an arrow should mark their normal direction of rotation. Make sure the tyres are marked as tubeless items. It goes without saying that, unless you plan to use your CBR solely on the track, both tyres should be road-legal, and not some racer's shredded cast-offs.

It would be nice to see a reasonable amount of tread on the tyres, of course, but the obvious truth – especially given the CBR's nature – is that that's not altogether likely. Who would fit brand-new tyres immediately before selling their bike? At the time of writing, United Kingdom regulations demand a minimum of 1.0mm (0.040ins) of tread over 75 per cent of the width of the tyre all the way round the tyre, and with no bald patches, but 2.0mm (0.80ins) is a safer minimum. Even so, be just a little suspicious if your prospective bike's tyre treads are this thin. What else might the owner have avoided spending money on?

At least, though, the overall wear pattern of the tread ought to give you some idea of how the bike is routinely ridden. Be a little wary, in other words, if the edges of the covers are worn as much as the middle; you might be buying not just someone's redundant trackday tyres, but their redundant trackday bike, too.

Electrics: lights, instruments

t should by now come as no surprise that the CBR's electrical system is almost 100 per cent reliable, and that any problems you do encounter will probably be due – as is so often the case – either to neglect or to misuse, or else to ignorant previous owners simply fiddling around where they've no business doing so. It's generally obvious if someone's been splicing into cables to add accessories, for instance. Look for stray insulating tape and cheap, crimp-on after-market terminals or, more worrying

Speedo can under-read, with obvious results, so it's well worth a check

still, Scotchlok-style connectors. Honda itself uses only top-quality male and female 'bullet' connectors with clear plastic shrouds.

That said, it is a relatively complex system, and it's worth a few minutes at least, perhaps with the help of the owner's handbook, to make sure that everything works more or less as it's meant to. That includes – obviously – all of the lights and the horn (including the instrument-panel warning lamps), and then the safety systems such as the side-stand interlock (designed to cut the engine if the stand is either extended or drops down while you're riding) and the gearbox/clutch safety switch (which prevents the engine starting in gear unless the clutch lever is pulled in). There's more on these in the relevant sections. And don't forget the alarm/immobiliser system, where fitted. Any caring and enthusiastic owner should be able to explain precisely how it's meant to function; someone who has stolen the bike that you're viewing may not.

The only specific issues we've come across are the possible failure of the voltage regulator on some earlier models (circa 1998), and then later (2004, 2005) failure of the generator itself. If it's the first the battery may be either undercharged or more likely overcharged; if the second it won't receive a charge at all, and will quickly go flat. Neither is a major problem to put right, however. Note that in some instances the sparks that result from the failure of the alternator windings can ignite the oil- and petrol-laden fumes within the crankcase, causing the camshaft-cover gaskets to blow out, and these will obviously need to be replaced at the same time as the generator.

As for the battery itself, it's a physically small 12-volt unit with quite a lot of demands placed on it (it's tucked away under the seat) and, whatever the condition of the generator and regulator, it won't last indefinitely. Make sure the terminals are tight and free from corrosion; that the electrolyte is at the right level. If in doubt simply budget for a good-quality new unit. Again, batteries aren't that expensive, and well worth almost any reasonable expense for the huge peace of mind they offer.

It goes without saying that all lights and other electrics should work!

Suspension and steering

Swinging arm gradually became a minor work of art in its own right

In order to assess the steering-head bearings you need either to park the bike on its side-stand or, better still, to support it with a jack and a block of wood under the engine (see the section headed What to take with you). Now sit astride the machine in the normal way, and attempt to pull and push the handlebars longitudinally back and forth (as opposed to rotating them from side to side). There should be no discernible movement. You might find it easier to have someone else move the bars, or to pull and push the front wheel back and forth, while you look closely at the relevant part of the frame, or perhaps feel for any looseness with your hand.

Now rotate the bars slowly from one lock stop to the other a few times. They should move freely and smoothly, with no obvious roughness or binding – and with no looseness, either. The clever electronic steering damper, fitted only from the 2004 model year, is designed to offer only a little resistance at low speed, but then to become progressively stiffer the faster you go. It has no particular faults.

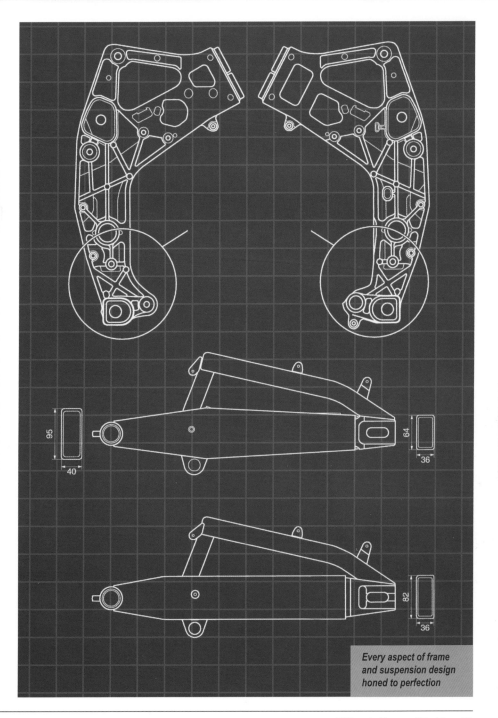

Every aspect of frame and suspension design honed to perfection

Steering-head problems are usually caused by the grease within either hardening with age or being washed out by over-enthusiastic use of a steam-cleaner. It may be possible to eliminate some or all of the looseness by adjusting the pre-load on the bearings, but this can only go so far. You'll probably need new ones soon. It's not a major drama to fit them, though.

No less important are the steering stops, the non-adjustable lugs on the frame and forks that limit the rotational movement of the handlebars. You'll find signs of normal wear and tear on the metal faces where they periodically (but only lightly) touch each other, but they're susceptible to damage – or even being knocked off altogether – if the front end of the bike sustains any kind of significant impact, and this makes this area of the machine a good indicator of its past life and treatment.

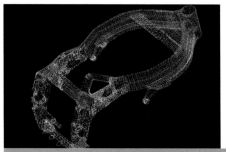

Uprated rear-suspension spring/damper unit is a popular modification, so too a steering damper for those bikes that didn't have one (bottom photo)

Frame and bodywork

The CBR's aluminium frame is in all cases a very substantial piece of kit, which generally stands up well to a remarkable amount of abuse, but there are none the less some fairly important points to note.

The biggest problem is that as a would-be buyer it's difficult for you to check whether it has ever been involved in a major accident. In certain cases it will be all too obvious – the bike may 'crab' as you test-ride it, although that might be caused simply by a misaligned rear wheel; see the Wheels and tyres section – but in others you may discover the unpalatable truth only after you've taken delivery. The best safeguard is either to buy an obviously good, cared-for bike from a reputable supplier, and let the warranty that you'll almost certainly get with it take care of any problems, or at the other end of the price scale to expect the worst and then, perhaps, to be pleasantly surprised.

Whether you go to the trouble of removing the fairing, the seat and the fuel tank, then, and inspecting the frame inch by inch, centimetre by centimetre, is up to you (and the bike's present owner, of course). In truth, the bodywork isn't that easy to take off, especially on later bikes, and many owners might object to such a major inspection in any case. But certainly both the seat and the tank are simple enough to remove. The front part of the seat is secured by two bolts, accessible by lifting the rear end of the cushion, and the tank is held on by another two bolts – one under the seat, and one (or in some instances, two) at the very front, just behind the handlebars.

Besides, you can quite easily examine the most vulnerable parts of the frame, as it were, without any dismantling at all. Check the front forks by applying the front brake and pumping the handlebars up and down. The suspension

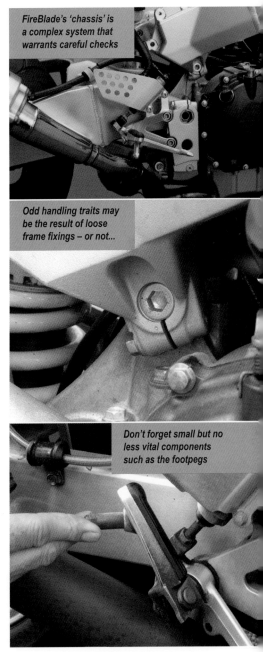

FireBlade's 'chassis' is a complex system that warrants careful checks

Odd handling traits may be the result of loose frame fixings – or not...

Don't forget small but no less vital components such as the footpegs

action should be smooth and linear, with no sign of the binding that could indicate bent legs, and definitely no sign of longitudinal scoring or corrosion on the plated working surfaces. You can expect to see a light film of oil on the fork tubes of higher-mileage bikes, but certainly no obvious major leaks.

Leaking seals aren't a major disaster, but it's a long and rather tedious job to replace them. On RR-Y to RR-3 models with upside-down forks there's also the possibility that the lower portion of either or both legs can crack. See the section headed Recalls for more information on this.

It's a similar story at the rear: bounce the seat up and down to check the single spring/damper unit for leaks (together with the remote-mounted pressure canister and hose), and make sure the damper is securely mounted both top and bottom, but at the same time appears free to pivot as required. It's also worth checking to see that the adjustable spring collars are free to turn, although for that

you'll need the appropriate 'C'-spanner.

Look for cracks in either the frame itself or its welded joints around the steering-head area. Again these suggest some sort of impact damage, but may also be the result of nothing more than repeated heavy landings after the rider has pulled a wheelie. Either way, you obviously need to do a little more investigation – or better still to find a bike that's been looked after rather more carefully.

The swinging arm supporting the rear wheel pivots on small-diameter ball races. Later bikes have the lighter – and stronger – Unit Pro-Link arm, designed to reduce unsprung weight and thus aid handling, but they're all exactly the same in principle. Check for free play by once again supporting the bike on a jack and a block of wood, and then pushing hard against each side of the rear wheel in turn. There should be no discernible movement. Note, though, that what might appear to be play in the swinging-arm bearings could be caused by worn or loose

wheel bearings. There's more on this in the section headed Wheels and tyres.

If there's either a little movement in the swinging-arm bearings or else a slight clicking sound, first check that the locknut for the swinging arm's pivot shaft is tight.

As a super-sports bike the CBR comes with only a simple side-stand rather than the full centre stand you'll find on a typical tourer, but it's none the less important to make sure that it works correctly. Examine the return spring for the loss of tension that could allow the stand to drop while the bike's in motion (have an assistant or the vendor hold the bike upright while you do so). Check also that the arm neither binds nor is so loose on its bearing – which cannot be lubricated – that the bike could even fall over while parked.

It's also important to check the functioning of the electrical interlock which is designed to stop the engine if the side-stand falls while the bike's in motion (but which, importantly, doesn't prevent the motor being started while it's parked on the stand; that's the job of the clutch lever/ gearbox interlock). Sit astride the bike, and then put the side-stand up and the transmission in neutral. Now start the engine, pull in the clutch, and select first gear. With the engine running, lower the stand with your foot in the normal way; the engine should stop as the arm deploys.

Damage to the bodywork is usually all too obvious – but not necessarily a major problem to put right, and so is potentially a useful bargaining point. The most likely causes are the bike being dropped, of course, which can give rise to all sorts of other issues, but poor home mechanics (you have to remove parts of the fairing for some of even the most basic maintenance tasks) can wreak all sorts of havoc.

It's less of a problem for the pre-1999 machines, with the panels secured by quick-

Crash buttons (above) may help prevent damage to engine (below) but make sure they haven't been over-tightened and cracked any of the castings

release Dzus-style fasteners, but Honda used Allen-style recessed-head fixings for the later bikes, and these are prone to seizing up if neglected. Look for signs of increasingly desperate attempts to undo them, and likewise give all the panels a gentle shake to make sure they're firmly attached. You really don't want anything working loose at high speed.

The good news is that the fairing comes in sections that can be replaced individually as required (most, if not all, are available from Honda, complete with precisely matching decals). The bad news, not altogether surprisingly, is that they're quite expensive for what they are, and especially by the time you've bought all the other little bits and pieces (rubber seals, screws, washers and so on) that you really need if you're to make the best job of it. And don't forget the windscreen, which if scratched or chipped will look a real mess.

1 All FireBlades should have an alphanumeric Vehicle Identification Number stamped into either the right- or the left-hand side of the steering head, and repeated on a riveted-on plate nearby. All these groups of letters and digits should match the bike's official documentation, and show no sign of having been tampered with. See also pages 26–29

2 On earlier models the bike's original colour scheme should be indicated by a coded adhesive label on the frame under the front part of the seat near the rear end of the fuel tank, and in later machines on a similar label in the small storage compartment beneath the rear seat/tail-light unit. For full details of this coding system turn to pages 30–32

3 Earlier bikes have a pull-out choke control on the steering head, and a cable operated clutch. On later machines cold starts are managed electronically, and the clutch hydraulically. The brake lever is simply adjustable for those with smaller hands. The gear-shift lever, on the left-hand side of the bike, is of the usual one-down-and-five-up pattern

4 All Blades have an 18-litre (4.5 US gallon) fuel tank with a modest 'reserve' supply built in. Octane should be at least 95, although it's best to use 98, especially if you ride the bike hard. Only later machines have a catalytic converter that requires the use of unleaded fuel only, but earlier bikes can still run on leaded gasoline

5 Earlier bikes had a 16-inch front wheel and tyre. While this sharpened up the steering, it was also said to make it feel rather twitchy sometimes. It's possible to fit a 17-inch wheel-and-tyre combination, though – usually from a later-model CBR600 – and this also gives a usefully wider choice of high-performance rubber

6 Essentially all Blades have two front and single rear rotors. Until the end of 2003 the front calipers were secured with side-facing bolts, but on 2004-model and later machines the bolts are rear-facing. Many owners fit after-market big-brake conversions, but the standard system is more than adequate for most road use

1 All Blades – and especially the later models, with their under-seat exhaust system – have a very compact rear end, with the single (fully adjustable) coil-spring/damper unit tucked inside the frame. Swinging-arm designs vary, too, but all are tough and reliable, and all have provision for easily checking and adjusting the tension of the all-important drive chain

2 Seat height and handlebar position vary in detail from year to year, but all can best be described as uncompromising. The low-set bars might give you neck ache (unless you're riding flat-out and gain some support from the wind), so try to have as long a test-ride as possible before you agree to buy. It's undeniably a bike best suited to shorter riders, too

3 Most components – tyres, brakes and hoses, chain and sprockets, exhaust and even the suspension and clutch – are far more readily accessible than in any sports car, and thus easy to inspect and look after as necessary. The engine, on the other hand, is rather hidden by the wraparound fairing, but both oil and coolant levels are still relatively easy to check

4 The FireBlade is both beautifully designed and built throughout, with superb attention to detail fit and finish. The massive aluminium frame, for instance, is a minor work of art in its own right. In most cases ready-painted replacements for the 'body' panels – even for the earliest bikes – are still available today

5 The CBR/FireBlade is badged as that only in Europe and some other countries; in the US it has always tended to be known by its engine capacity alone: hence CBR918RR, CBR929RR, CBR954RR and finally CBR1000RR. Don't worry, though: they all perform and handle like the race-bred thoroughbreds they so plainly are

6 No less controversial than the earlier Blades' 16-inch front wheel was the absence of any form of steering damper. This shouldn't be a problem for all but the most determined of riders. Honda didn't fit a steering damper until the 2004 model year, when it equipped the bikes with a clever self-adjusting electronic device

What to look for – at a glance

1 Engines vary in capacity, but none has any major weaknesses. Regular oil and filter changes are essential, so check history for evidence. The most likely transmission problem is jumping out of gear, and clutches can slip, but both are easy to fix. Weakest link is the chain and its two sprockets – but again these are easy both to inspect and then replace

2 Check fuel system for leaks, especially from flexible hose under tank, which in earlier machines could be stretched. Rough idling and poor throttle response may be due to worn or out-of-balance carburettors, or to perished rubber diaphragms. Later fuel-injected bikes are very reliable in this respect. Check that turning the handlebars has no obvious effect on idle speed

3 Make sure rotors and pads aren't excessively worn. Check fluid level in reservoirs, and that the pipework is both sound and routed correctly. Both wheels and rotors have arrows to show they're fitted the right way round. Check bearings for excessive play by shaking wheels from side to side. Tyres must no less obviously have a good tread depth and the right speed rating

4 Make sure oil-pressure warning light comes on and goes out as it should, and also that side-stand interlock works properly: if running, the engine should cut out as you lower the stand with your foot. There's also an interlock to prevent the engine being started with the transmission in gear unless the clutch lever is also pulled in

5 Front and rear suspension should compress and rebound smoothly, and there should be no leaks from either the fork seals or the single rear damper. Steering-head bearings can dry out and become loose, but this will be obvious if you support the bike with the weight off the front wheel and attempt to rock the handlebars longitudinally

6 Check the frame for obvious signs of major impact damage – cracks, dents or other distortion – and make sure steering-lock stop on either side of headstock is marked only lightly. Heavier marks – or even a stop that's missing – suggest the bike has been 'dropped'. Make sure frame's identification number(s) is/are present and correct

APPENDIX

Data and useful information on the web

There are literally hundreds of CBR websites on the internet. We cannot endorse any one of them, but the list shown here should at the very least get you started.

www.world.honda.com/motorcycle
Official Honda motorcycle's world website, technical papers

www.powersports.honda.com/motorcycles/sport/
Official Honda motorcycle website with bike descriptions

www.honda.co.uk/motorcycles
UK importer's website

www.motorcycle.com/honda
Useful information source/foums

www.cbrforum.com
Enthusiast website

www.motorcyclenews.com
Reviews and comment from well-known British weekly magazine

www.cbrfirebladers.co.uk
UK enthusiast website

www.honda-fireblades.co.uk
UK enthusiast website

www.totalmotorcycle.com
Motorcycle specifications, comparisons

www.onyerbike.net
CBR dealers, and a valued contributor to this guide

www.hpicheck.com
UK-based site for pre-purchase identity/history checks

www.vehiclelicence.gov.uk
UK site for checking basic details/status of any UK-registered vehicle

ABOUT THE AUTHOR

C hris Horton has been a motoring writer since the mid-1970s, and a full-time car journalist since 1978, when he left his job in a bank to become assistant editor of the UK's long-running *Car Mechanics* magazine. He followed that with a short period as editor of *Kit Cars & Specials*, and then worked on both *Sports Car Mechanics* and *Classic Car Mechanics*, becoming editor of the latter in 1985. He spent most of the next 10 years on several other classic-car titles, eventually becoming editor-at-large of the popular and much-missed *Your Classic*. In 1994 he took over as editor of the then newly established *BMW Car*, and in 1996 was appointed editor of *911 & Porsche World*, a position he held until turning to life as a freelance at the beginning of 2006. He remains a consultant editor to *911 & Porsche World*, and also now edits the online quarterly *Rover Enthusiast*.

Chris owns a large collection of both cars and (Honda) motorcycles, including at least six classic Rovers, three BMW 5-series sedans, two Porsche 944s and a Volkswagen LT panel van. His bikes – the majority dating from the mid-1960s – include three CB160s, a CB72 and a CB77, a C72, and last but not least a rare CB450 'Black Bomber'. He also owns a 1956 BSA B31, today in the process of being completely rebuilt, and as a direct result of writing this book is currently negotiating the purchase of a 1995 FireBlade. Chris, together with his wife and cat, and most (but by no means all!) of the above machines, lives in Oxfordshire.

Chris Horton
E-mail: porscheman1956@yahoo.co.uk

Acknowledgements

To Steve Brockbank at independent dealer On Yer Bike near Aylesbury, in England; to photographer Peter Robain, and not least to Stuart Yardley, general manager at official dealer Abingdon Honda, near Oxford, England. Stuart in particular was an enthusiastic source of much valuable information. Many thanks also to Nic Turner, who runs the popular cbrfirebladers website (www.cbrfirebladers.co.uk) and Ian Ward, whose superb 1995 Urban Tiger is shown in a number of the photographs.

Ultimate Buyers' Guides include:

- Porsche 911 Carrera (964) 1989 to 1994; ISBN 978 0 954999 04 9 (2nd Edition)

- Porsche 911 Carrera, RS & Turbo (993); ISBN 978 0 954999 01 8 (2nd Edition)

- Porsche Boxster and Cayman, all models 1996 to 2007; ISBN 978 0 954999 06 3 (3rd Edition)

- Porsche 911 Carrera, Turbo and GT (996); ISBN 978 0 954999 07 0 (2nd Edition)

- Porsche 944 and 968; ISBN 978 1 906712 07 5

- Porsche 911, the classic models (1964 to 1989) incl Turbo and 912; ISBN 978 0 954999 09 4

- Porsche 911, all models including Turbo and GT (997) 2004 to 2009; ISBN 1 978 906712 00 6

- MGF and TF; ISBN 978 0 954557 96 6

- Land Rover Discovery; ISBN 978 0 954557 97 3

- Subaru Impreza; ISBN 978 0 954557 98 0

- Honda CBR900RR & CBR1000RR FireBlade; ISBN 978 0 9549990 3 2

Plus:
Porsche Boxster and Boxster S; Introducing the world's favourite roadster. DVD. Running time: 70 minutes, PAL colour format, region code 0 (all regions, but not USA)